Soul Plan and Soul Contracts

Decode Your Soul's Mission Through Numerology, Astrology, Akashic Records, Spiritual Communication, and Secret Wisdom

© Copyright 2025 - All rights reserved.

The content contained within this book may not be reproduced, duplicated, or transmitted without direct written permission from the author or the publisher.

Under no circumstances will any blame or legal responsibility be held against the publisher, or author, for any damages, reparation, or monetary loss due to the information contained within this book, either directly or indirectly.

Legal Notice:

This book is copyright protected. It is only for personal use. You cannot amend, distribute, sell, use, quote, or paraphrase any part, or the content within this book, without the consent of the author or publisher.

Disclaimer Notice:

Please note the information contained within this document is for educational and entertainment purposes only. All effort has been executed to present accurate, up-to-date, reliable, and complete information. No warranties of any kind are declared or implied. Readers acknowledge that the author is not engaging in the rendering of legal, financial, medical, or professional advice. The content within this book has been derived from various sources. Please consult a licensed professional before attempting any techniques outlined in this book.

By reading this document, the reader agrees that under no circumstances is the author responsible for any losses, direct or indirect, that are incurred as a result of the use of the information contained within this document, including, but not limited to, errors, omissions, or inaccuracies.

Your Free Gift
(only available for a limited time)

Thanks for getting this book! If you want to learn more about various spirituality topics, then join Mari Silva's community and get a free guided meditation MP3 for awakening your third eye. This guided meditation mp3 is designed to open and strengthen ones third eye so you can experience a higher state of consciousness. Simply visit the link below the image to get started.

https://spiritualityspot.com/meditation

Or, Scan the QR code!

Table of Contents

INTRODUCTION 1
CHAPTER 1: UNDERSTANDING SOUL CONTRACTS AND PRE-BIRTH AGREEMENTS 3
CHAPTER 2: WHAT IS MY PURPOSE? 19
CHAPTER 3: NUMEROLOGY AND THE SOUL: DECODING YOUR LIFE PATH 30
CHAPTER 4: ASTROLOGY AND THE SOUL PLAN: HOW THE STARS ALIGN WITH YOUR DIVINE PURPOSE 49
CHAPTER 5: EXPLORING THE AKASHIC RECORDS TO FIND YOUR MISSION 67
CHAPTER 6: CONNECTING WITH GUIDES AND HIGHER BEINGS FOR CLARITY 77
CHAPTER 7: THE ROLE OF KARMA AND PAST LIVES 87
CHAPTER 8: CREATING YOUR SOUL PLAN 98
CONCLUSION 108
HERE'S ANOTHER BOOK BY MARI SILVA THAT YOU MIGHT LIKE 110
YOUR FREE GIFT (ONLY AVAILABLE FOR A LIMITED TIME) 111
REFERENCES 112
IMAGE SOURCES 113

Introduction

Everyone has wondered, at least once, if there was more to life than what meets the eye – if there was a point to every encounter and every happenstance.

Why do bad things happen? Why do good things happen? Is there a grand plan or purpose guiding your steps, even if you can't always see them? The concepts of soul contracts and soul plans sound a bit esoteric. However, whether you believe in them or not, they're thought-provoking and could show you a few things about your soul's mission on earth – why you're here.

The book title caught your attention, so perhaps you have a basic understanding of soul contracts, or deep down, you know there's more to this existence than what everyone else sees on the surface. There's a pull, a yearning to find and follow the elusive threads found throughout time and, of course, your life – and this book will help you understand it all.

A soul contract is a proposal, an agreement you made with your higher self before you were born. This contract contains the lessons, relationships, and experiences you committed to exploring in this lifetime. And your soul plan? It's the navigational system or compass that helps you fulfill the contract.

Why does life feel so complicated sometimes if all this planning was done beforehand?

If you're contemplating this, then you're asking the right questions. In this book, you'll learn the nature of soul-level agreements, how to identify your contract's major components, how to work with your energy, and how to align with your soul's highest intentions.

Many books are available on this topic. However, you may find their approach a little dry or academic. But not with this book. You'll notice a more hands-on, interactive feel that teaches you to establish a better connection between you and your spiritual self than ever before.

You won't need two books to understand the twin concepts of soul contracts and soul plans. Not when everything you need is right here, in one thoughtfully crafted volume. Both concepts are inextricably linked, and when you understand the big picture, the *"why"* of your life experiences, the cycles, joys, and hardships, they form part of a conscious, divinely engineered display with you at the center.

Chapter 1: Understanding Soul Contracts and Pre-Birth Agreements

It is believed that long before you took your first breath, your soul – the eternal, non-physical you – went through intense, meticulous preparation. You sat down (metaphorically) with your higher self, spiritual guides, and other souls you're destined to meet and devised a plan for your journey to Earth. This is called a soul contract.

Soul contracts are energetic agreements.[1]

Soul contracts are energetic agreements made before incarnating into this physical plane. Before you run away screaming at the thought of more paperwork, soul-level agreements are not the legalese you'd find in a standard contract. They are cosmic, a divine to-do list of your higher self noted from pure inspiration. The language is direct, the terms are non-negotiable (at least by your ego), and there's not a single clause about late fees.

Humans overcomplicate things. However, your higher self operates on a different frequency with access to the big picture. They can see your journey's perfect map from that expansive vantage point – the necessary relationships, lessons, and opportunities that will catalyze a rebirth, your transformation. Knowing what they know, they drafted your soul contract, complete with every ingredient you need to accomplish your soul's destiny.

Things get complicated once you incarnate and get absorbed into hustle culture.

Many things are required daily, including many societal constructs that you must abide by as a member of society. As expected, you forget about your pre-planned agreements at birth, and life has a way of burying your destiny underneath the rubble of human existence. Your ego takes over, and you are led astray from your soul's true purpose. Luckily, your higher self anticipated this. They knew you'd get swept up in the chaos the moment you opened your eyes. They saw it coming – the drama, the social obligations, and the intrusive thoughts – but won't leave things to chance. They're always one step ahead and built-in little breadcrumbs and trail markers to help guide you back to your soul's true path.

Suppose you get these nagging feelings or inexplicable connections with certain people. In that case, it's a part of your soul contract being activated. You may have a friend you've known since you were in diapers, and don't talk to them anymore, but never delete their number. Or maybe there's one coworker who gets under your skin, for better or worse. Or you've experienced an inescapable pull towards a person, even when logic says you should be running in the other direction? How many times have you met someone and felt an immediate connection, like you've known them for lifetimes? More often than not, these are manifestations of your soul contract.

When you open your eyes to the divine orchestration of your relationships and life story, the irritating tension with your younger sister is no longer pointless drama but an opportunity to learn patience. That dead-end job you got fired from could be your reminder to stop settling and chase your dreams. Regardless of whether it has been scientifically proven, this perspective takes you out of a victim mentality and redirects you to find meaning and clarity in your life.

The Purpose of Soul Contracts

- **Lessons:** A guru or shaman will tell you that this is the real reason we're all here. Your soul contract is a personalized curriculum tailored only for you. They lead you to and through good and bad experiences necessary for your consciousness's growth and expansion.
- **Karmic Balancing:** Karma . . . the cosmic IOU that keeps on giving, right? Through your soul contracts, you can settle outstanding karmic debts or relationships from your past lives. You can forgive and be forgiven by those you've previously crossed paths with. You get a do-over, although what you do with it is ultimately your choice.
- **Soul Purpose Alignment:** Your soul purpose covers everything you are meant to do in this lifetime. It is the path your soul is destined to follow. Your soul contract puts up signposts on this path to keep you en route. This route should take you to the people, places, and encounters that will help you fulfill your divine calling and become the highest version of yourself.

Your soul purpose is to find the right path.³

- **Relationship Dynamics**: Your soul contract stipulates the connections you'll have with the important people in your life. These connections can be a karmic bond to a romantic soulmate. They create the conditions for the lessons you'll learn together and the resulting growth experiences.
- **Spiritual Transformation**: Despite what is written in your soul contract, you have free will. You can choose not to honor your contract's details. However, if you live in alignment with it, you're essentially inviting the universe to shake your foundations. Your entire life goes from black-and-white to full-blown technicolor, and it is the most beautiful yet bittersweet experience. All roads lead to your soul's purpose. You can ignore the directions and carve your own path. Still, soul contract coordinates exist for a reason that you will only understand if you follow them.

The Elements of a Soul Contract

- **Birth and Early Life Experiences:** The circumstances surrounding your birth- such as the time, location, and family into which you are born- are intentionally chosen and stipulated in your soul contract. Childhood experiences, including your family relationship, traumas, or significant events, are intentional because they shape your personality, emotional patterns, and karmic lessons.
- **Karmic Lessons:** Karmic lessons are major themes or lessons your soul has agreed to work through during this lifetime. These lessons are usually based on unresolved issues or imbalances from your past lives, which you've brought forward to address and eventually transcend. They are not pretty, but that's usually the point, or you may never confront your fears and learn the lessons.
- **Karmic Relationships:** These are the connections you agreed to revisit in this lifetime to work through lingering issues, heal old wounds, and, most importantly, shed negative patterns. Relationships like these are intense, charged, and hardly ever peaceful. They conjure your deepest fears, insecurities, and triggers – what you need to confront and integrate to break free from the cycle of karma.

- **Soulmate Connections:** When people think of soulmates, they immediately consider a romantic partnership with two people who fit together in a way that makes sense. They're not wrong. However, soulmate connections can show up in other forms, like a best friend, a role model, family, or a familiar stranger. There's always recognition, understanding, and resonance between soulmates, regardless of their form. You feel like you've known this person for ages, even if you've just met them. There's an effortless flow to the relationship, an intuitive communication beyond words. While not karmic, these relationships will test you, push you out of your comfort zone, or reveal parts of yourself that you've kept hidden.
- **Tests of Faith and Perseverance:** Life will test you. There's no need to sugarcoat it. There will be periods of uncertainty that test your persistence, patience, and strength of character. However intense they may feel, these tests are not random or arbitrary. They are carefully designed teaching moments put on your path to help you transcend old limitations and stretch the boundaries of your consciousness. It is part of the grand, multidimensional syllabus you signed up for.

Pre-Birth Agreements

Before you were incarnated on this planet, you existed somewhere else, as pure consciousness, in a non-physical, spiritual place. This version of you is your higher self. It was here, in this formless state, where you intentionally plotted the parameters of the life that you were about to undertake on the physical plane. It was here that you thought of the main narrative arc, character development, and important themes of your storyline.

A significant part of this pre-birth process is establishing soul agreements, pacts you make with other souls who have important roles in your future life. These pacts could be contracts with family members, lovers, close friends, mentors, or rivals. They create the relationships and exchanges that form the optimal conditions for your spiritual growth and fulfillment of your soul's agenda.

Your soul agreements aren't rigid or set in stone because, within the agreements, you have free will. You're not doomed to have a difficult relationship with everyone you enter a soul agreement with. For example, your rivals or enemies aren't necessarily there to drive you crazy. They might, but that's not the point. They may have agreed to play that role to force you out of your comfort zone, trigger epiphanies, or push you to address lingering inner conflicts. Regardless, how you respond to these people and situations is up to you.

Another pre-birth agreement involves your relationship with your physical vessel - your body. Your soul carefully selects the genetic, energetic, and circumstantial makeup of its human form. Factors like your gender, ethnicity, natural talents, and weaknesses - and even the time and place of your birth - are consciously chosen to serve the soul's evolutionary agenda. Your body is the vehicle that carries your soul through this lifetime, so your soul puts a lot of thought and intention into selecting the right form for its mission. Your body is a manifestation of your soul's intentions.

Outside the agreements you make with the souls incarnating with you, your higher self actively seeks out ascended masters, angelic guides, and other highly evolved consciousnesses to guide and support you. They are your spirit guides. This invisible network is always available, whether or not you're aware of its presence. They have access to perspectives and knowledge transcending the physical world. When you open yourself to their guidance, you receive signs and synchronicities that point you in the right direction.

Interplanetary and Extraterrestrial Pre-Birth Agreements

Your astrological birth chart might tell you which and where planets were at the time of your birth. However, the soul agreements you made prior to incarnation include more than the celestial bodies in the solar system. Your soul contract carries the fingerprints of other planetary and star systems.

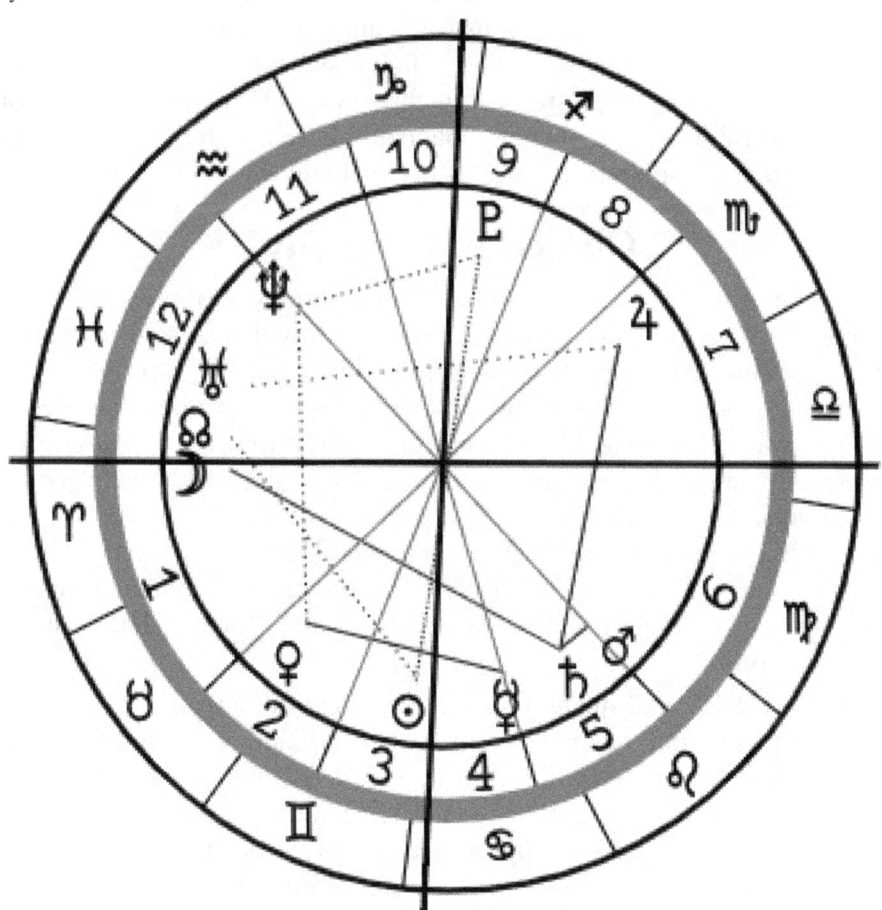

Birth charts can tell you about your alignment with the universe.'

Every person has the same elements created in the belly of dying stars billions of years ago that have been found in everything on Earth. Science has proven this. You are, in essence, a child of the universe.

Some people feel a strong, mysterious connection to ancient Sumerian symbols or lunar cycles or something well beyond the solar system. These could be signs that their soul's pre-birth agreements involve close ties to planetary archetypes and star systems far outside Earth. Best-selling author and medical intuitive Caroline Myss explained that the energetic imprints of celestial bodies, including ones far away, can reveal much about your soul's evolutionary journey. For example, those with strong Sirian influences might feel called to teaching roles, wisdom-sharing, and humanitarian service. Whereas Venusian energies may find expression through artistry, beauty, and loving relationships. Arcturians are known for being gifted healers, peacemakers, and pioneers of cutting-edge spiritual technologies. While these are not rigidly deterministic, and many people could have ties to more than one-star system, it doesn't hurt to ask, "What do I feel called to?"

Choice and Destiny

Since humanity can recall, philosophers, theologians, and ordinary people have racked their brains for answers to the age-old question: Does free will exist, or is life predetermined by a higher power or force? Is fate a matter of choice or destiny? These questions are deep, complex, and perennial. The implications of how they are answered can irrevocably alter human's understanding of life, purpose, and place in the universe. If there is true free will, then you bear responsibility for your actions and the trajectory of your life. However, if everything is predetermined, then how much control does anyone genuinely have? Are people merely puppets dancing to the forces that eclipse comprehension?

Weighty existential quandaries like these can tie anyone's brain into knots, and the older you get, the more complicated and mind-boggling they become. When you were nine, the answers were clear-cut. "Duh! I have free will. I do what I want every day." Then life comes at you, and setbacks set in. Tragedies and unanticipated redirections make you question whether you're in the driver's seat. Life is like the old saying, "We plan, and God laughs."

Choice implies agency, the capacity to decide and direct the course of your life. Whenever you choose, you exercise free will – the power to select options and do only what you want. Free will suggests that the future is not set in stone but malleable based on your choices in the present.

Alternatively, destiny insinuates a predetermined fate or course of events completely out of your control. It means there is a higher power, God, the universe, or another force that has already mapped out your entire life. So, no matter what choices you think you're making, you are only playing out a script that has already been written. Your life stops being the product of your volition. It is the unfolding of a plan set in motion long before your parents were born.

So, Which Is It, Choice or Destiny?

According to many spiritual and philosophical traditions, the answer is in the soul's flexibility and intentionality. The soul is not bound by rigid destiny but instead returns to life with specific experiences and lessons it hopes to experiment with and master. Despite this, the soul maintains the freedom of how it responds to those experiences.

Is life about choice, destiny, or both?[4]

In the video game *Detroit: Become Human*, you follow the stories of three humanoid androids in a futuristic timeline where artificial intelligence has developed self-awareness and emotions. Despite their programming to fulfill certain functions, these androids soon figure out that they can make choices that determine their lives and the course of human-android relations. This game has multiple endings, each determined by the choices you, the player, make.

This reference explains the symbiotic relationship between predetermination and free will. You may feel bound by your genetic programming, upbringing, or societal conditioning, but your capacity for conscious choice and free will defines who you are and what you become.

Will you surrender to your base impulses? Will you give in to fear at every turn? Will you rise above the limitations of your circumstances? You own a good portion of the responsibility for the choices you make. You can't always blame your genes, childhood, or culture for your outcomes. The buck stops with you. You are your story's author, come what may. So, what will you do with the gift of free will?

Choosing Your Destiny

Everyone knows about intuition. However, no one, not even science, has figured out how it works. You know why it works but not necessarily how. Essentially, intuition is rapid, unconscious information processing. The brain can draw upon past experiences, accumulated knowledge, and muted environmental cues to produce or inspire quick insights and hunches - typically before you're even consciously aware. Picture your mind as an iceberg. The conscious, logical mind is only the tip, while the majority of your mental activity happens below the surface, subconsciously. Intuition originates from this subconscious database filled with stored information and pattern recognition, which is how you make snap judgments and decisions without understanding their full rationale.

Your mind is like an iceberg, with visible and invisible traits.[5]

Humans aren't the only ones who possess intuition. Birds know when to migrate. A dog senses danger before its owner does. A dolphin can detect sickness. A Border Collie knows how to herd animals. How? They can't tell you, but these are examples of intuition in action.

Humans are only as instinctive as animals in the animal kingdom but ignore or distrust that part of themselves in favor of their logical, rational minds.

Intuition is the soul's preferred method of communication. Not everyone can always consciously articulate the reasoning behind their intuitive hunches. However, those gut feelings are direct communications from the subconscious mind, and that part of you is aware of your soul contract and the unfolding of your soul's journey.

You have free will, but you can use this free will in alignment with your soul's mission – a mission you are being guided to intuitively. The more you trust your intuitive wisdom, the easier it becomes to discern between the authentic choices of your soul and those driven by more superficial, egoic impulses. Not all your hunches will be intuitive. Sometimes it's fear or anxiety. You can separate wisdom from your ego's chatter *and* live in sync with your destiny, *and* co-create your life in partnership with your soul's higher intelligence with meditation, mindfulness, and other spiritual practices.

Questionnaire: Understand Your Soul Contract

1. What are the predominant themes or patterns consistently showing up in your life despite the changes or transitions you go through? These should point you to potential lessons or soul-level agreements for this lifetime.

   _____
   _____
   _____
   _____
   _____
   _____
   _____

2. Are there particular situations or problems you repeatedly deal with, even if the details are different? Maybe you keep dating the same types of people, even when you choose a different "type," or you keep trading one addiction for another. These could be the manifestation of unfinished business within your soul contract. Answer:

3. Are there recurring emotional states, behaviors, or thought patterns that refuse to leave you alone?

4. What are the foundational values, beliefs, or principles that have been steady guides for your choices?

5. Consider the relationships that matter the most to you. They could be your boyfriend, girlfriend, spouse, best friend, family, etc. Are there common themes between them? If yes, what are they?

6. Are there specific archetypes or roles people always play in your life, even if they have nothing in common? For example, are your friends always the caretaking, authoritarian, or defiant types?

_____
_____
_____
_____
_____
_____
_____

7. Looking back at your relationships, what lessons do you think you were meant to learn? Is there a major lesson those relationships were trying to teach you?

_____
_____
_____
_____
_____
_____
_____

8. Do the issues in your relationships mirror the internal work you need to do? How?

_____
_____
_____
_____
_____
_____
_____

9. When you think about the biggest transitions and turning points in your life, what are the common themes?

_____
_____
_____
_____
_____
_____
_____

10. Are there particular character archetypes, symbols, or motifs that recur in your life and dreams? It could be more than one. Archetypes are categories for characters representing universal traits or ideas that are easily recognizable. Character archetypes include the wounded healer, the trickster, the magician, the sage, and the orphan.

_____
_____
_____
_____
_____
_____
_____

11. How do these archetypal energies and themes relate to the lessons you think you're here to learn?

_____
_____
_____
_____
_____
_____
_____

12. How are these themes and archetypes expressed in your outer life? How are they expressed in your psychological and spiritual environment?

_____
_____
_____
_____
_____
_____
_____
_____

13. What are the most persistent problems in your life?

_____
_____
_____
_____
_____
_____
_____
_____

14. Do you think these problems are related to your growth and purpose? How?

_____
_____
_____
_____
_____
_____
_____
_____

15. In what area of your life do you feel stuck? Where can you identify the most resistance? Is it in your career, finances, health, self-image, or self-expression?

_____
_____
_____
_____
_____
_____
_____

16. What lessons must you master to free yourself from these blockages?

_____
_____
_____
_____
_____
_____
_____

Chapter 2: What Is My Purpose?

From the wealthiest person in your neighborhood to the homeless guy down the street, everyone wants to feel that their lives are fulfilling and have meaning. This search for meaning and fulfillment is a universal human desire, but it's also highly personal to each person. What does it mean to live a fulfilling life? What is meaningful and fulfilling in life? Meaning leads to a purposeful life. A meaningful life contributes value to the world, and fulfillment signifies contentment, satisfaction, and self-actualization. The two are closely linked, yet it's possible to have one without the other. Some people find their lives meaningful but not especially fulfilling. Others may feel fulfilled but struggle to pinpoint the greater meaning of their lives.

What does a meaningful life consist of?[6]

Isn't it easier to live life freely without a concern for what the point is? Where does this drive for meaning and fulfillment come from? Some say it's the intrinsic human need for connection, importance, and transcendence. Humans are social creatures who love belonging and feel a strong need to affect their environment somehow. People are hardwired to ponder the big questions of existence – why are we here, what is the nature of consciousness, is there a higher power or higher purpose? The answers involve a lot of self-reflection, experimentation, and trial and error. Some turn to religion or spirituality, hoping to find meaning through faith and connection to the divine. Some find meaning in their work, relationships, creativity, or service to people. Others feel stuck with existential angst, not knowing if there is any true meaning to be found.

Searching for More

It's not always easy to differentiate between genuine spiritual or existential longing and restlessness or boredom. Today, society rewards productivity and material success above all else, so admitting to this need for purpose can feel like admitting weakness. Still, the search for meaning has inspired the greatest works of art, scientific discoveries, and some of the world's most influential philosophies and religions. Do you know your purpose? How can you be sure that your life isn't meaningful or fulfilling? How do you know you are searching for more?

The most common signs are:

- **Restlessness and Dissatisfaction**

This comes with a dull sense that something is missing, even when your life looks generally successful or comfortable. You could be daydreaming about quitting your job or fed up with the daily grind. Persistent dissatisfaction is usually a sign that your soul is searching for something more meaningful and in line with your calling and values. You can push these feelings aside all you want and tell yourself to be grateful for what you have. However, it doesn't change the truth about what your soul wants.

- **Repetitive Daydreams**

Sometimes, your mind wonders about alternative lives or missed opportunities. However, when these daydreams refuse to go away, you may need to pay attention. What are your imagination's themes? Are you fantasizing about fame, a specific industry, spending more time with friends, or a radical shift in how you spend your time? Your repetitive daydreams might be breadcrumbs leading you to your purpose.

- **Lack of Meaning and Purpose**

In the many components that constitute your life – your work, relationships, pastimes, and daily routine – do you find meaning and purpose? Or are they more of a means to an end, a way to get through the day? As you can guess, mundane activities can be filled with much meaning if they give your life purpose. On the other hand, if your life feels like mindless repetition, it may be time to reevaluate what you think your purpose is.

- **Flow and Timelessness**

Do you remember the last time you were so absorbed in an activity that you didn't notice time zooming by? What were you doing? Were you singing, painting, coding, or out with your best friends? Losing time in mid-activity means you were in the flow state. When you're in this zone, your enthusiasm and concentration become effortless. If you don't have activities where you can lose yourself, you may be lacking in purpose.

- **The Desire to Make a Positive Change**

Many people want to leave a positive legacy. They want their lives to matter; they want to contribute something meaningful to their community and the world. You may feel the same way. You're drawn to causes, organizations, or lifestyles for a palpable effect because you desire a purpose.

- **Spiritual or Existential Curiosity**

For many, the search for more is directly tied to meaning, purpose, and the truth about existence. It's the big question: Why are we here? What happens when we die? Is God real? Curiosity about the universe's mysteries has led many to contemplate philosophies, religions, or paths to self-discovery in the pursuit of answers and their purpose.

What Is My Purpose?

Nobody's purpose is neatly packaged and presented to them on a silver platter or a fixed destination. There will always be something to discover about who you are and what you have to offer the world if you are patient, curious, and willing to figure it out. In most cases, the initial impulse is to look outward – to look for purpose in work, your roles, or your effect on the environment. Undoubtedly, there's value in that. When you feel your life is making a meaningful contribution through your career, volunteering, or raising a family, it feels like your life means something. However, the search for purpose requires looking inward, too. Who are you? What do you value? What are you afraid of? Outside what society has labeled success, what makes you truly happy?

Purpose doesn't have to be grand or earth-shattering. Sometimes, it's as small as kindness, creativity, or presence - the parent working tirelessly to give their child the world, the artist who communicates through their art, the kind soul working in hospice. An ordinary life can have an extraordinary meaning.

Purpose isn't static or singular. It is bound to shift and change as you move through different stages of life. What felt meaningful in your 20s may feel different in your 40s or 60s. You grew, so you should adapt. You're not the same person you were five or ten years ago. Your priorities have shifted. Your purpose is inseparably linked to personal growth and evolution. As you mature and become more experienced, your perspective on what matters may expand or change entirely. No, you haven't gone out of alignment with your soul. You're unfolding gradually and beautifully, like a flower. What seems different and out of alignment might be that you are *more in alignment* than ever before.

Becoming aligned could mean disorientation, uncertainty, and existential crisis. You may question everything you believe. You may doubt your choices and get lost in the maze of life. However, if you are strong enough to sit in the discomfort, do what you must, and trust the process, you will realize that your soul is taking you precisely where you must be.

Autonomy and Self-Determination

The 21st century is marked by technological advancement, global interconnectedness, and the domination of large institutions threatening autonomy and self-determination, *whether people admit it or not.* Every day, you are assaulted with messages from the media, advertisers, corporations, friends, and family, telling you how you should live. There's so much pressure to conform, climb the corporate ladder, and get rich no matter what it takes at the cost of your values, even if the cost is yourself.

Society is slowly but surely inching toward a hive-mind mentality as more people lose touch with their freedom, intuitive wisdom, and authentic self-expression. The temptation to just go along with it and avoid rocking the boat is so strong, especially when the consequences of bucking the system are public shunning and physical threats. Is it possible to balance free will and a soul contract when the cultural narrative is hell-bent on conformity and compliance? The answer is absolutely.

Society is now living with a hive-mind mentality.[7]

The human soul is wired for freedom – freedom to express, to create, and to be. Your free will isn't an accessory to humanity. It is the foundation upon which your soul contract rests. Your soul contract requires active, conscious participation because the more you cede your directorial control to outside forces, the more the vision gets diluted, and the point gets lost.

You may be drawn to a random book or podcast for no apparent reason, only to discover that their message is precisely what you need to hear. You get an idea or inspiration that feels like it was downloaded into your brain from outside of your conscious mind. Or someone gives you something seemingly useless that you need at the next minute.

The orchestrated perfection is unmistakable when living in attunement with these discreet, energetic signals. Things that felt like a mere coincidence or random chance become a puzzle piece to a more intelligent design. You can no longer deny that everything is happening for you, not to you, and helping you manifest your highest purpose.

All you have to do is commit to honoring your truth and walking the road less traveled. In recognition of your courage, the universe responds in kind, opening doors, manufacturing possibilities, and sending you the people, resources, and wisdom you need when you need them most. When you're aligned with your soul's purpose, you can trust that there's a method to the madness, even if you can't see it yet.

Tools and Practices for Uncovering Your Purpose

Boredom Is Not Always Bad

Boredom has become a dirty word. Every minute must be filled with stimulation, doom scrolling on social media, binge-watching TV shows, and rushing from one obligation to the next. The slight prospect of being alone with your thoughts for more than a few minutes fills many with nameless dread.

Modern life is frenetic. People are so overstimulated that they've forgotten how to listen to themselves. There is always a distraction. It's your phone notifications going crazy or the many "must-dos" on your to-do list causing your soul's still, small voice to get drowned out. More people need to intentionally make space for stillness and silence if there is a hope of giving that small voice a chance to be heard. It's in the emptiness when you suppress the impulse to reach for your phone or turn on the TV that you hear what your soul is telling you.

This is a tough sell in today's restless, productivity-obsessed culture, conditioned to see idleness as a moral failing, a wasted opportunity, and a problem to solve. What's the worst thing that could happen if there was nothing but you and silence? What if it holds the answers you seek about who you are, why you're here, and how you're meant to serve?

Journaling

The thought of sitting down to write in a journal is scary, the fear reserved for homework and office presentations. Who would think that the answer to "What is my purpose?" could be at the bottom of a pen?

Journaling can open the windows to your soul."

Contrary to popular opinion, writing in a journal is not stuffy or rigid. It can be wonderfully fluid and creative. Write down your thoughts, even the *"dumb"* ones. Write down your dreams, especially those you're too afraid to tell anyone. Write down your wishes, particularly those that feel so out of reach. Write it all down. Don't think too much about the wording, if it's organized, or if it makes sense. Your journal is a mirror. Only one pair of eyes is staring into it, yours. Nobody else is looking. What do you like? What don't you like? What happened yesterday, and how did it make you feel? Pick any of the following prompts and see where it takes you:

1. Describe your perfect day from start to finish.
2. What are you most grateful for right now?
3. Make a list of 10 things that make you happy.
4. Write about a childhood memory that makes you smile.
5. If you could travel anywhere in the world, where would you go? Why?
6. What are your biggest fears? Do you think you can get over them? How?
7. Describe your dream job or career.
8. Write a letter to yourself. What three pieces of advice would you give yourself?

9. If you could change one thing about the world, what would it be?
10. Think about the most difficult problem you recently had. How did you handle it?
11. Write about five things you're passionate about. Do they have anything in common?
12. Write about a time when you felt most alive.
13. Describe your ideal apartment or house. What does it look like?
14. How do you typically deal with stress and anxiety?
15. Write about the best relationship you've experienced. It doesn't have to be romantic.
16. Describe your perfect date night or weekend getaway.
17. What talent do you wish you had? Why?
18. What do you wish you had more time for?
19. Have you achieved anything recently that you're proud of? Write about it.
20. If you could have a superpower, what would it be, and how would you use it?

Forget about finding the right answers and focus on being honest with yourself. Don't censor yourself; this isn't Instagram. Be raw, real, and unapologetic. It's how you figure out who you are and what you're here to do.

Meditation

Meditation is another way to connect with your soul and reveal your purpose. Everyone meditates differently. Some prefer to sit quietly, cross-legged, eyes closed, and focus intently on their breath. Some meditate better when they can move their bodies, like in walking meditation or light yoga. Others weave a little meditation into their regular activities, like doing laundry mindfully. Some people don't like to meditate. Who can blame them? Sitting like a yogi for hours doesn't sound like something anyone who isn't a yogi would want to do.

Thankfully, you're not a yogi, and you don't have to meditate like one to reap the benefits of this ancient practice. Meditation has evolved because people have evolved, but the end game is the same: to know yourself and to find inner peace. There is a guided meditation exercise below. However, you can meditate as you like. Every meditation has three markers that are adaptable to any preference. They are:

- **The Starting Point:** This is the part of your session where you get comfortable, preferably somewhere quiet. It could mean sitting down, lying down, going for a walk, starting your chores, etc. As long as it is a beginning that feels natural, not forced, it'll work. This is where you consciously decide to step away from the outside world and go inward.

- **The Journey:** This is the meat of the practice, where you focus on whatever you want, as long as it is repetitive. You can focus on your breath, an affirmation, or your body's sensations. Your mind is likely to wander; it happens to everyone. Gently guide your attention back to what it was focused on initially. It gets easier the more you practice.

- **The Landing:** You're at the end of your session, where you rejoin the world. You can take a few deep breaths, take a shower, eat, go out for some fresh air, or do whatever you need to integrate the peace and clarity from the concluded session.

If your session hit all three stages, congratulations, you just meditated. It doesn't matter if it was for five minutes, 10, or 30 - you meditated. Here is a guided meditation session for finding your purpose:

1. Get a comfortable seat. It can be on the floor, or if you prefer to lie down, go ahead. Allow your body to settle, and gently close your eyes. Set the intention of finding your soul's purpose. Know that this is the session's purpose.

2. Breathe in deeply once, twice, three times. With each exhale, release tension and distractions.

3. Imagine standing in a beautiful forest. The sunlight is filtering through the trees, the leaves are brilliantly green, a soft moss is beneath your feet, and you hear insects buzzing.

4. This forest represents your soul. Feel how peaceful it is. There is much wisdom in this place.

5. Begin walking through this forest. Take your time, look around, smell the air.

6. Keep an eye out for thoughts, images, or feelings that come to you. Don't force anything; trust your soul and let it lead the way.

7. Walk toward an ancient tree in the middle of this forest. It's up to you how far or how close this tree is. This tree represents the wisdom and guidance of your higher self. It knows your true purpose. Do you trust this tree? Do you feel safe around it?
8. When you feel safe, sit at the base of the tree and converse with it. What questions do you have about your life's purpose? What is the tree telling you?
9. Listen closely and freely. Don't try to manipulate the answers to fit what you want to hear. Know that the answers you seek are already within you.
10. When you're ready, slowly make your way out of the forest.
11. Take a few deep breaths and open your eyes.

Surrender to the Unknown

By now, you must know that everywhere you look, there is some advice on how to *"find your life purpose."*

You could say the same thing is happening right here, right now. Everyone is exchanging elaborate methods, long checklists, and step-by-step formulas to help you find your calling. Undoubtedly, these approaches are helpful for some. However, many are still lost, even after doing everything. What about doing nothing? How about a different process – one that's more about letting go than trying to control? Why force the issue and relentlessly pursue a predetermined idea of what your purpose should be when the wisest path may be to surrender to the mystery? You keep stressing and strategizing, but what if you just let go instead?

Surrendering and going with the flow might feel counterintuitive, especially if you're used to being in the driver's seat. Everyone has achieved something or is working hard toward achieving something, so the thought of loosening your grip and trusting the process could seem irresponsible. As scary as it is, you need to permit yourself to slow down and see what life is presenting you. What if you allowed yourself to be surprised, to follow unexpected breadcrumbs, and to say yes to things you never would have predicted?

Stop hunting down your purpose and let it find you. No, this doesn't translate to sitting back and doing nothing. There's still action required on your part, although the action looks a little different. This time, you must stay present and committed without attachment to an outcome.

Trust that the answers will reveal themselves in due time. Don't see it as doing *"nothing."* You're choosing receptivity over-reactivity, and sometimes, that's all your soul needs from you. When the answers and opportunities come, and they will, you'll know what to do.

Chapter 3: Numerology and the Soul: Decoding Your Life Path

The entire universe is a giant mathematical formula. Everything that exists can be reduced to a mathematical formula inside a mathematical formula.

At the most fundamental level, the building blocks of all life – subatomic particles, forces, and fields – are governed by the rules of mathematics, and it doesn't stop at the smallest scales. The movement of planets, stars, and galaxies obeys the principles of mathematics according to classical mechanics and general relativity. Phenomena such as planetary orbits around the sun, the expansion of the universe, the propagation of light, and the atoms forming the cells in your body can be predicted and explained using mathematical formulas.

Numerology is a great tool to help decode your path.'

This undeniable connection between mathematics and reality gave birth to numerology, the study of the mystical and symbolic relationship between numbers and the physical world. Numerologists believe that everything can be reduced to a single-digit number, from 1 to 9. These numbers have powers and properties influencing people's lives, personalities, and experiences.

The History of Numerology

Numerology is popular today thanks to one man, Pythagoras. Pythagoras was a philosopher living in ancient Greece. Although he was born and raised there, he wasn't quite as Greek as history books would have you believe. His father was a Phoenician, and the Phoenicians were famous throughout the ancient world for seafaring and extensive trading networks. This Phoenician connection is in part responsible for how Pythagoras grew up because, as intelligent as he was, knowledge was very scarce in his time.

As the son of a wealthy Phoenician merchant, he had access to rooms, information, and people that were unheard of for the average ancient philosopher. Through his father's contacts and trading relationships, Pythagoras could study under the greatest minds in the ancient world, including Thales of Miletus, a few Egyptian high priests, Babylonian rabbis, and Themistoclea, a Delphi oracle. He rubbed elbows with Persian magicians, Phoenician kings, and Chaldeans, who were great thinkers and sages. These great minds were a long way from home for Pythagoras. Hence, it was this broad, cross-cultural education that led to his revolutionary ideas about numbers.

Pythagorean Numerology Table

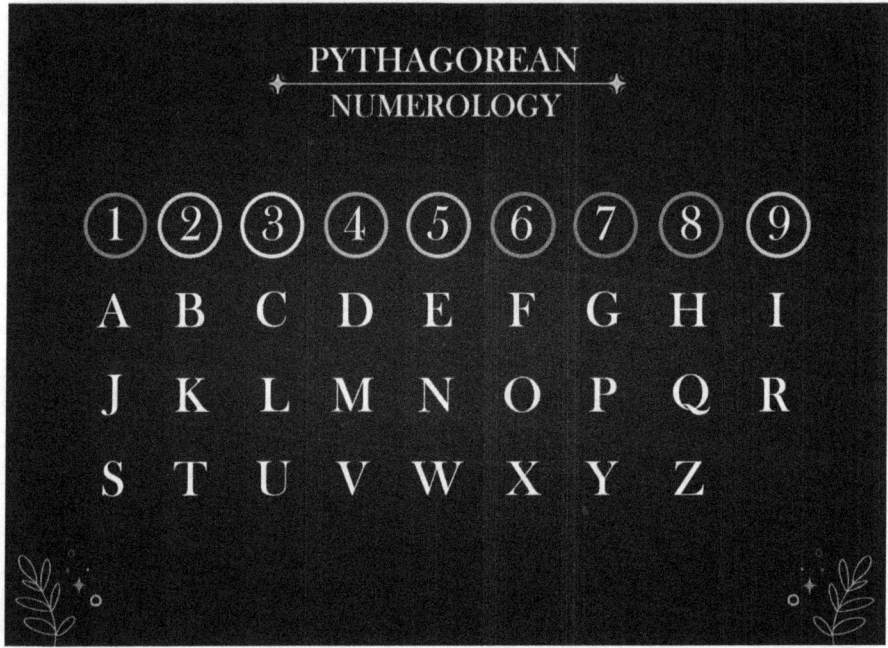

Pythagoras was convinced that there was a divine, numerical code embedded in all creation, and it was his mission to crack it. He started a school with this in mind, and the numerical implications of your name determined if you were admitted or not. Too far? Maybe, maybe not. Pythagoras wasn't the only one who believed that numbers could predict everything, even personalities. The Chaldeans were already doing this long before Pythagoras was born.

Chaldean Numerology

The Chaldeans were an ancient Mesopotamian people in Babylon, modern-day Iraq. Over 4000 years ago, they developed a system that assigned numerical values to their alphabet letters based on their position and frequency within the language. They believed that using these numerical values could predict a person's personality, talents, and destiny using only their name. Back then, people used nicknames, while their legal names remained a closely guarded secret to protect their destiny. Only mothers knew their children's real names.

Chaldean Numerology Table

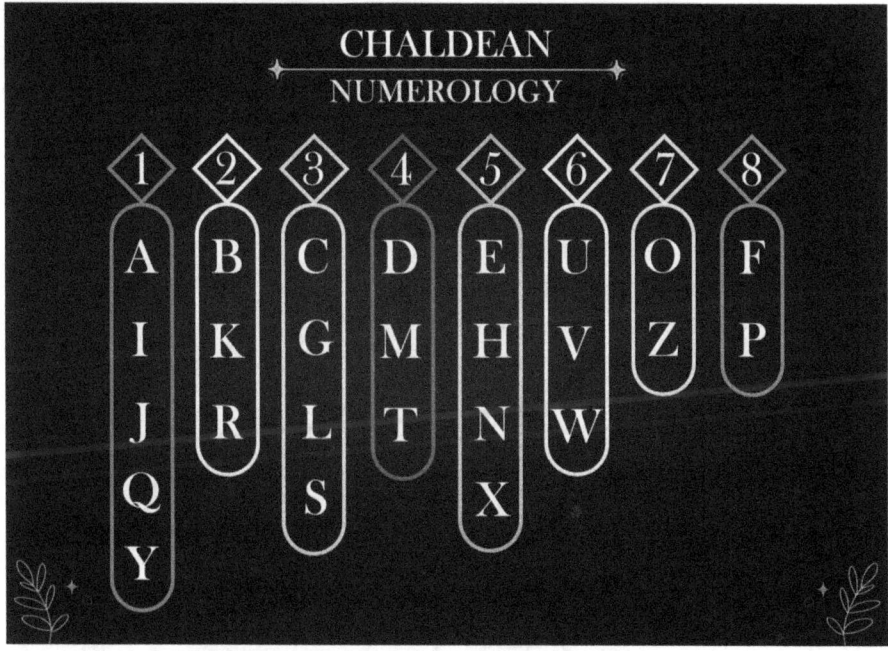

This numerology system became available to the Greeks after Alexander the Great invaded and conquered Babylon. If not for Chaldean numerology, the Pythagorean system never would've existed. Chaldeans believed that everything in the universe vibrates - produces invisible ripples or waves - and, like instruments, everything has a signature vibration. They understood that synchronized vibrations attract each other, and likewise, unbalanced vibrations attract the same.

Another interesting Chaldean belief is the predestination of life. They believed, without a doubt, that every life is a pre-written script and its destiny is set in stone, waiting to play out.

Sounds a lot like soul contracts. But 4,000 years ago? The Chaldeans thought that the numbers associated with the letters in your legal name and the numbers in your full birth date reveal your vibrational signature. This signature determines your life's course, your personality, your talents, and your destiny's defining milestones. Try as you might, you can't change the plot - your destiny is locked in from the minute you're born. You can see why it made sense to keep your birth name a secret in those days.

The Chaldeans figured out that you could tweak your script a little by changing your legal name. Destiny doesn't seem so locked in now, does it? According to this ancient civilization, if you officially change the letters of your identity, you could potentially alter its vibrational frequencies and partially rewrite said destiny. They were onto something because, to date, the Chaldean system is more precise and reliable than most forms of numerology.

Numerology and Other Mystical Traditions

Apart from Chaldean numerology, one of the oldest and most influential numerology traditions comes from the Jewish Kabbalah. Kabbalists were obsessed with the divinity in numbers, especially the first 10 numbers, which they believed to be divine emanations that created the universe.

Each of these 10 numbers, called the Sephirot, had a personality and meaning. For example, the number 1 symbolizes unity and new beginnings. The number 3 represents the balance between mind, body, and spirit. Number 7 represents perfection and spirituality. One of the earliest Kabbalistic works, the Sefer Yetzirah, explains the symbolic meanings of the first 10 numbers and how they relate to the 22 letters of the Hebrew alphabet. For these mystics, numbers weren't just neutral – they were portals straight to the divine. This practice is called *Gematria*.

The Sephirot.[10]

The Jews weren't the only ones with something mystical to say about numbers. Numerology has been essential in Eastern cultures for centuries. The Chinese associate the numbers 1 through 9 with elements, directions, and philosophical principles. The number 8 is a lucky Chinese number because its Chinese name, *"ba"* rhymes with *"fa,"* which means good fortune. This is not secret knowledge; the 2008 Beijing Olympics opening ceremony took place at 8:08 pm on 8/8/08. Meanwhile, the number 4 is treated like the plague because they believe it represents bad luck and death.

Ancient Egyptians were interested in numbers. They were into a lot of things, but numerology was as important to them as it was to other corners of the world. It can only mean one thing: numbers are as important as they are mysterious; *be the missing piece to understanding your soul's purpose.*

Spiritual Meaning of Numbers

- **Number 1: The Leader**

    Number 1 centers around new beginnings, individuality, and taking the lead. It represents the pioneering spirit, innovation, and the need to blaze your own trail. Spiritually, the number 1 means self-reliance, confidence, and manifestation. It's a reminder to trust your intuition and fearlessly go against the grain.

- **Number 2: The Peacemaker**

    The number 2 embodies harmony, balance, and cooperation. It's the number of diplomacy, partnerships, and fairness. Spiritually, 2 represents the yin and yang, the divine feminine, and unity. If you see the number 2, you are being encouraged to be open-minded and empathetic and to work with others for the greater good.

- **Number 3: The Visionary**

    Number 3 symbolizes creativity, self-expression, and the mind. It's the number of the artist, the dreamer, and the visionary. Spiritually, 3 stands for the divine trinity, the life-giving force of the universe, and manifestation. Seeing this number should inspire you to communicate your truth, imagine more, and share your talents with the world.

- **Number 4: The Builder**

    The number 4 is structure, stability, and the practical application of ideas. It represents the builder and the organizer and brings order to chaos. Spiritually, 4 means protection, the four elements, and the need for discipline and diligence in everything you do.

- **Number 5: The Adventurer**

    Number 5 represents adventure, freedom, and a thirst for something new. It is for the explorer, the seeker, and those who embody change. Spiritually, it is used to represent the five senses and divine grace. It's a reminder to step out of your comfort zone, surrender to the unknown, and live life to the fullest.

- **Number 6: The Caretaker**

    This is the number of the caretaker and the healer who brings balance and healing. Spiritually, 6 represents the divine feminine, unconditional love, and the responsibility to care for others and the planet. It is compassion and safety for yourself and others.

- **Number 7: The Seeker**

    Number 7 is known worldwide for perfection. It is the number of spirituality, introspection, and the search for purpose. It is for the mystic, the philosopher, and the mysteries of the universe. Spiritually, it represents divine wisdom, intuition, and human connection with the unseen. It's a number that inspires you to go within, to question your beliefs, and to seek the truth that exists past the physical world's veil.

- **Number 8: The Manifester**

    Number 8 signifies abundance, power, and manifestation. It's for the entrepreneur, the leader, and those who have mastered the material world. It represents the infinity symbol, divine balance, and the mastery of the spiritual and earthly domains. This number encourages you to step into your power, use your resources wisely, and create a legacy.

- **Number 9: The Humanitarian**

    Number 9 symbolizes universal love and the desire to serve humanity. It's for the humanitarian, the visionary, and those who see the big picture. Spiritually, 9 represents divine completion, spiritual maturity, and transcendence. It's the number for altruism and a reminder to leave the world a better place than you found it.

Karmic Numerology

Karmic numerology is not very popular because karma has a reputation for being "bad," and people would rather not pour their energy into negativity. However, karma is not inherently bad. It doesn't mean you are a bad person. It means you have a few lessons to learn and karmic debts or unresolved issues from past lives that are carried over and manifested in your current life.

Your karmic number is only there to help you identify the unhealthy cycles and areas you agreed to work through in this lifetime so that they don't follow you into your next life. Karma is heavy, but the lessons are necessary, and the quicker you drop the baggage, the faster you can move on, light as a feather.

In karmic numerology, the two main branches are karmic lesson numbers and karmic debt numbers.

Karmic Lesson Numbers

Your karmic lesson number is any number that is missing from the numerology of your full legal name. The missing numbers represent a skill or trait that is lacking or weak, a void you must fill. For example, suppose your name is Smith Darius Wilson. In that case, your numerology will be *1 4 9 2 8 4 1 9 9 3 1 5 9 3 1 6 5*, starting from the first letter in your first name to the last letter in your last name. Looking at these numbers, only one number is missing, number 7. So, your karmic lesson number is 7. Some people don't have karmic lesson numbers, but that doesn't mean they don't have karma. Remember the other branch of karmic numerology: karmic debt number.

For those with karmic lesson numbers, here are your karmic lessons for this lifetime:

- **Number 1:**

  If you're missing the number 1, you could have problems taking charge and decision-making. You might wait for people to tell you what to do instead of taking the initiative. Your life lesson is to become more self-motivated and confident. You'll need to stand up to strong-willed people who try to control you and stop procrastinating.

- **Number 2:**

    With a missing 2, you need to work on being more cooperative and considerate. You may prefer to stay in the background instead of putting yourself out there. Your lesson is to learn diplomacy, patience, and how to be a team player. Consideration of how your actions affect those around you will help you build stronger relationships.

- **Number 3:**

    If your karmic lesson number is 3, you may be extremely self-critical. You might struggle with imposter syndrome or think you've done a terrible job even when others are impressed. Your lesson is to accept that no one is perfect and become more optimistic. Be proud of whatever you do, even if it isn't flawless.

- **Number 4:**

    Without a 4, you could feel lost and uncertain of the right life path to take. You must work on being more organized, disciplined, and grounded. Finding the right job or career might be tricky, but when you find it, stick with it and put in the hard work because it will pay off.

- **Number 5:**

    For a karmic lesson 5, your lesson is to become more adventurous and adaptable. You probably don't like to try new things or step out of your comfort zone. You need to stay receptive to change, take risks, and have faith that you can handle whatever life throws at you.

- **Number 6:**

    A karmic lesson 6 has commitment issues. You may run away or keep people at arm's length because it feels safer. Your lesson is to learn how to build and sustain serious, genuine relationships. You must learn vulnerability.

- **Number 7:**

    For a karmic lesson 7, you must develop your talents and reach mastery at whatever you do. You might prefer only to skim the surface of things. Your lesson is to put in the time and effort to master a skill or subject that speaks to you.

- **Number 8:**

  A missing 8 has the potential to be financially successful, but you may not be very good at managing your money. Your lesson is to learn your limits and find balance. Don't take on too much risk, or you could have trouble holding onto your wealth.

- **Number 9:**

  You need a lesson in compassion. You need to find ways to stay connected to the world around you. Sometimes, you must take the spotlight off yourself and consider the greater good. Think of the bigger picture and make sacrifices for your community.

Karmic Debt Number

The choices you make and how you live have consequences that carry over from one life to the next. Your karmic debt number represents the vibrational energies of these consequences. It is calculated using your full birth date. Unlike the karmic lesson number, this number is derived from the numbers that are present.

Karmic debt numbers are from 13 to 19. So, if your full birth date adds up to any of these numbers, you have a karmic debt number. Each number's meaning is:

- **Number 13:** If you have a 13 karmic debt, you're someone who puts a lot of effort into everything you do. You're a hard worker, but sometimes, you may not like this about yourself because it feels like there's always something in your way, no matter how hard you try. You might have felt tempted to give up many times. Ironically, many successful people have a 13 karmic debt, but they made it because they kept going and remained focused. Focus doesn't come easy to karmic debt 13s. Their attention is almost always spread out across too many projects. They jump from one thing to the next and never give anything their full effort. It's where they run into trouble. If this is you, you need to pick a goal and stick to it. Forget about taking shortcuts. The easy way out hardly ever works for 13s. Stay organized, keep to a schedule, and follow through on what you start. That's your lesson.

- **Number 14:** Karmic debt 14s misused their freedom in the past. Now, they're being forced to adapt to unexpected changes and random occurrences. They're at risk of turning to unhealthy coping mechanisms like drugs, alcohol, or overindulgence, so another life lesson is moderation. If you're a karmic debt 14, you have no choice but to be flexible and adaptable. Life has thrown you too many curveballs already, and it doesn't look like it's slowing down. You will need to take life as it comes, but still keep your eye on your goals. If you want something, you need to want it badly enough to stay committed even when you're repeatedly redirected. Keep your goals high and your indulgences low. Above all, don't give up on your dreams. It's okay to be afraid, but trust that the redirections are taking you where you want to go. Don't take your eye off the prize, and don't give up.

- **Number 16:** This karmic debt is transformation and renewal. The old self must be torn down to make way for the new. Karmic debt 16s are deep thinkers and highly intuitive people. They have the potential for great spiritual growth but run the risk of egoism and looking down on others. They are prone to alienation and loneliness. The 16 teaches you to let go of the structures and beliefs that have kept you separate from your true self and higher consciousness. It might be a painful process, watching the collapse of the life you've built, but on the other side of the destruction is a rebirth. With the 16, life will keep presenting you with choices and situations that force you to let go of your grand plans and ambitions. It's frustrating, but it's part of the process. Be humble and trust your intuition, but also be practical in how you apply your wisdom.

- **Number 19:** Karmic debt 19 teaches you about hyperindependence and the responsible use of power. You may experience many situations where you're forced to stand up for yourself and go it alone. One of your main lessons in this lifetime is to work through your stubborn resistance to accepting help. You want to be self-sufficient so badly that you forget everyone and everything is connected and interdependent, no matter how much you might want to be an island unto yourself. You must find the right balance between independence and connection. You need to learn that it's okay to rely on someone else and receive help. You don't have to do everything on your own. You're a risk taker, and there's a saying among risk takers, "If you want something done well, do it yourself." This is true, except that even the most independent and capable people need help sometimes. Ask for help; otherwise, your independence quickly becomes a prison.

Master Numbers

Master numbers are special life path numbers. They are different, not because they are identical double digits but because of the digits. Master numbers are 11, 22, and 33 because of the numbers 1, 2, and 3. Other identical double digits – 55, 88, 44 – are also special. However, they are power numbers, not master numbers, and not life path numbers.

People with master numbers are extraordinary, but with great power comes great responsibility. Here's what this means:

- **11:**

    Master number 11s are the messengers or the illuminators. This number has been tied to intuition, idealism, and spiritual enlightenment. Generally, anyone with 11 as a master number is extremely sensitive, empathetic, and plugged into the spirit world. Their heightened awareness connects them to higher planes of consciousness. They are natural healers, teachers, and visionaries who inspire and assist others. The 11s are known for their creativity, imagination, and appetite for knowledge, but they also carry a heavy burden. The increased sensitivity of this number makes them prone to anxiety, overthinking, and feeling almost drowned in the world's energy. They may have a hard time with self-doubt, insecurity, and perfectionism. Despite their mastery, the 11s must learn to balance the spiritual and the practical – and the intuitive and the logical. They must learn to manage their sensitivity and find practical applications for their gifts or risk being swallowed by them. They might be conduits of light and wisdom, but they need stability and balance in the physical world.

- **22:**

    Master number 22, typically called the "master builder" or the "master manifesto," is the most powerful of the three master numbers. It is known for ambition, leadership, and big dreams. People with 22 as a master number are natural problem-solvers and strategists. They have an eye for detail and the foresight to plan for the long term. The 22s are practical and organized. They take an idea and transform it into something tangible. They don't believe in limitations; if they don't have the resources, they'll find them. This is a blessing and a curse because the 22s also suffocate under the pressure of their potential. The high expectations they set for themselves and the world cause burnout, stress, and inadequacy. It's never enough for a 22, but they need to learn that, sometimes, it is. Some 22s are controlling or obsessive in their quest for perfection. There is a balance between ambition and compassion, and every 22 needs to find it. They must learn to delegate, trust others, and make time for self-care.

- **33:**

The 33s are the master teachers and healers. This number is associated with unconditional love, universal wisdom, and commitment to service. The 33s feel a chronic desire to help people and make the world a better place. They are the teachers, counselors, and guides, which explains their extraordinary patience, empathy, and understanding of the human experience. However, the weight of their responsibilities can quickly become too much for them to handle. They may experience burnout, not be very good at setting boundaries, and will almost always overextend themselves. The 33s must learn to balance their need to serve with the need to honor themselves. Their love and selfless service must be grounded in wisdom because no one can pour from an empty cup.

Core Numbers in Numerology

Life Path Number

Your life path number is the most important part of your numerology report. It reveals your life journey and purpose. To figure out your life path number, add the digits in your birth date, then reduce that sum to a single digit.

For example, if you were born on March 15, 1985, your calculation would be:

3 *(for March)* + 15 *(for the day)* + 1 + 9 + 8 + 5 *(for the year)* = 41

4 + 1 = 5

So, someone born on March 15, 1985, would have a life path number of 5.

Each life path number, from 1 to 9, has identifiable themes and characteristics.

- **Life path 1s** are natural leaders. They are confident, decisive, and unafraid to take charge.
- **Life path 2s** are diplomatic and sensitive. They value peace, empathy, and cooperation.
- **Life path 3s** are creative and expressive. They are charismatic, friendly, and optimistic. They enjoy entertaining or inspiring people.
- **Life path 4s** are practical, detail-oriented, and hardworking. They like structure, organization, and getting things done the right way.
- **Life path 5s** are adventurous and adaptable. They love new experiences, freedom, and variety. The 5s get bored with routine and are always eager to try the next new thing. They are curious, spontaneous, and open-minded.
- **Life path 6s** are nurturing and responsible. They want nothing more than to care for people and make a positive difference in the world.
- **Life path 7s** are introspective and analytical. They like to know things. The 7s are private, contemplative, and drawn to spiritual or intellectual activities.
- **Life path 8s** are extremely goal-oriented. If they understand anything, it's business, leadership, and material success. The 8s are ambitious, disciplined, and bold.
- **Life path 9s** are compassionate, empathetic, and idealistic. Like 6s, they want to make the world a better place and might prefer creative, artistic, or service-oriented roles.

Expression Number

This core number is calculated using your full birth name (first, middle, and last) and represents your natural talents, skills, and potential. To know your expression number, you take the numerical value of each letter in each name, add them, reduce the numbers per name to a single digit, and then reduce that to a single digit.

Using the name Harvey Reginald Specter as an example, the calculation would be:

$H(8) + A(1) + R(9) + V(4) + E(5) + Y(7) = 34$.

$3+4=7$

$R(9) + E(5) + G(7) + I(9) + N(5) + A(1) + L(3) + D(4) = 43$

$4+3=7$

$S(1) + P(7) + E(5) + C(3) + T(2) + E(5) + R(9) = 32$

$3+2 = 5$

$7+7+5=19$

$1+9=10$

$1+0=1$

So, the expression number for Harvey Reginald Specter would be 1. Here's what each expression number means:

- **Number 1:** Number 1s are very independent and confident. You're not afraid to take risks and try new things. You prefer the freedom to make your own decisions.
- **Number 2:** Number 2s are more intuitive and sensitive than most. You seek out balance, and you'd rather resolve conflicts peacefully. You're good at working with others, but you get thrown off by negativity.
- **Number 3:** You're outgoing and optimistic, with a creative, uplifting energy. People find you inspiring. You're drawn to the arts or other expressive outlets, but don't let yourself become too cynical, irresponsible, or undisciplined.
- **Number 4:** Number 4s are practical, methodical, and grounded. You're a reliable and responsible person. You come off as very stable with family and at work. You're also very stubborn.
- **Number 5:** With a number 5, you likely love freedom, excitement, and everything new. You're an adaptable free spirit who makes it a point to avoid routines and social norms. You also change your mind too often, get bored too quickly, or leave things unfinished.

- **Number 6:** 6s are loving and honest. In any circle, you're always the healer or counselor. You are the most likely to sacrifice your time and energy to care for the people around you. To some people, this comes off as too overprotective or an inability to stay out of other people's business.
- **Number 7:** 7s are as inquisitive as they are intelligent. Always on the hunt for truth, knowledge, and wisdom, you're more introverted and prefer having your own space and alone time to work on your projects. People might complain that you're secretive or disconnected.
- **Number 8:** Expression number 8s are ambitious, disciplined, and hardworking. These qualities, along with your planning skills, attention to detail, and realistic foresight, always lead you to great success.
- **Number 9:** Number 9s are interested in anything that promises to make the world a better place. You're idealistic, humanitarian, and a visionary. Don't let yourself be taken advantage of.

Personality Number

Your personality number is the filter through which the world sees you, at least at first. It's the impression people get when they first meet you or if your interactions are surface-level. Your personality number influences the energy and characteristics you put out there. It determines the people and information you're drawn to and the information you're comfortable putting out into the world.

Your personality number is calculated with the numerical value of the consonants in your full name.

So, Harry James Potter's personality number is:

H(8) + **R**(9) + **R**(9)= 26

2+6= 8

J(1) + **M**(4) + **S**(1)= 6

P(7) + **T**(2) + **T**(2) + **R**(9)= 20

2+0= 2

8+6+2= 16

1+6= 7

Harry's personality number is 7, and each personality number has a distinct meaning.

- **Number 1:**

  You come across as ambitious and confident. People see you as someone who knows what they want. Still, you need to be careful not to seem too egotistical or intimidating.

- **Number 2:**

  You have a friendly and trustworthy energy. People are attracted to your warmth and approachability. You're the one they come to for help, but you must watch for indecisiveness or being seen as a pushover.

- **Number 3:**

  You are charming and creative. Your wit and optimism are your most attractive qualities, but you must be cautious that you don't come off as superficial or exaggerated.

- **Number 4:**

  People see you as reliable, organized, and great at getting things done. They trust your judgment and knowledge, especially in business. However, try not to be too serious or predictable.

- **Number 5:**

  You have a daring and passionate spirit. People find you inspiring, but some might think you're too aloof or superficial.

- **Number 6:**

  Your personality is warm and caring. You're everyone's go-to for emotional support. As agreeable as you are, you need to ensure you're not being taken advantage of.

- **Number 7:**

  Your aura is more reserved and intellectual. People respect your intelligence but find it hard to get to know the real you. Try not to appear too opinionated or arrogant.

- **Number 8:**

  You project a strong, ambitious, and confident energy. You are a capable leader and good decision-maker. However, some might think you are egocentric or greedy.

- **Number 9:**

    Your charisma is your selling point. People love your idealism and positivity, but there's a risk of seeming too arrogant or above others.

Soul Urge Number

The final core number is the soul urge number, called the heart's desire number. This number reveals your heart's desires and motivations. To calculate the soul urge number, you take only the vowels in your full birth name (including Y if it produces a vowel sound when the name is pronounced) and add their numerical values.

Using Harry James Potter as an example again, the calculation would be:

$A(1) + Y(7) = 8$
$A(1) + E(5) = 6$
$O(6) + E(5) = 11$
$8+6+11 = 25$
$2+5 = 7$

The soul urge number for Harry James Potter is 7.

Here are the meanings of soul urge numbers from 1 to 9:

- **Number 1:** Soul urge number 1s are independent and motivated to be in charge.
- **Number 2:** Number 2s want harmony, peace, and security.
- **Number 3:** 3s are creative, imaginative, and sociable.
- **Number 4:** 4s find comfort in routine, structure, organization, and stability.
- **Number 5:** Number 5s long for freedom, variety, and new experiences.
- **Number 6:** 6s are motivated by compassion, empathy, and sacrifice.
- **Number 7:** 7s are introspective and introverted.
- **Number 8:** 8s want authority and influence.
- **Number 9:** 9s are idealistic and philanthropic.

Applications of Numerology

- **Making Decisions**

  Numerology can help with decision-making. For example, deciding between two job offers. Say one is with a company that has the expression number 7, and the other is a company with the expression number 3. Suppose 7 fits better with your numerological profile. In that case, there's a good possibility that the role and work culture is a better fit for your strengths and tendencies. The number 3 company may be too social and extroverted unless that's what you're looking for. This numerological information could help you make the best choice for your success.

- **Choosing Dates**

  Your wedding date is an important decision. You want to pick a day that will bring good luck and usher you into a happy marriage. You can choose the best date by calculating the numeric value of potential wedding dates. This will tell you what days of the month have the most favorable numerological qualities for your wedding or other events.

- **Understanding Your Relationships**

  The dating scene is chaotic. If you want an idea of your romantic compatibility from the start, you can calculate the numeric values of both your names. You may learn that while your profiles have some good synergies, the numeric relationship between you has a hidden 8 energy, which could mean power struggles and control issues. Now, you can have a healthy conversation with your person about setting healthy boundaries and communication patterns to nip this potential friction in the bud.

- **Timing Is Everything**

  Mostly, it's not how you do a thing – but when. Assuming you're preparing to ask your boss for a raise, you can check the numeric value of the upcoming week to know what energies will be at play. Then, you can strategically schedule your meeting for the best day, knowing that the numerological influences will be working in your favor. This timing could give you an extra edge and increase your chances of getting what you want.

Chapter 4: Astrology and the Soul Plan: How the Stars Align with Your Divine Purpose

Looking up at the sky, you could think you're a small, insignificant speck compared to over 100 billion galaxies and even more stars that fill the sky. However, astrology is evidence that the universe is anything but impersonal. Astrologers believe that the positions and movements of planets, stars, and constellations are more influential on human affairs than we think. They're not wrong. There is order beneath the apparent chaos, even if nobody fully understands it. Scientists might disagree; they see the universe as a large, mechanical system governed by the laws of physics. They're not wrong, either. The universe is so unimaginably massive that humanity may never understand. Astrology is a 5000-year-old system that hasn't failed yet. Something about it defies skepticism. If not, horoscopes would've gone extinct, and nobody would care about their natal chart.

The stars are relevant to your soul purpose.[11]

Skepticism aside, nothing is still, even according to science. Stasis doesn't exist. Everything is always spinning and interacting with everything else. Your body, objects, plants, animals, and the ground beneath your feet might look stationary, but they're not. Since there is movement on Earth, so is there movement in the sky, with the planets, stars, and other celestial bodies perpetually orbiting and shifting. The macrocosm and microcosm are so interconnected that what happens in the stars above customarily reflects on the earth below, and your natal chart is this interconnectedness made manifest. It is a concrete and detectable proof of movement in the heavens. Your natal chart shows you precisely where every celestial body was when you were born. Each position carries an energetic imprint replicated in the different facets of your life.

Components of the Natal Chart

Sun Signs

When interpreting and understanding a natal chart, the sun sign is treated as the most important and defining aspect of the entire chart. Your sun sign, which is determined by the sun's position at your birth, is the essence of your astrological personality.

Astrologically, it determines your identity and how you choose to express yourself externally. It represents your ego, your will, your intensity, and your purpose. So, what does your sun sign say about you?

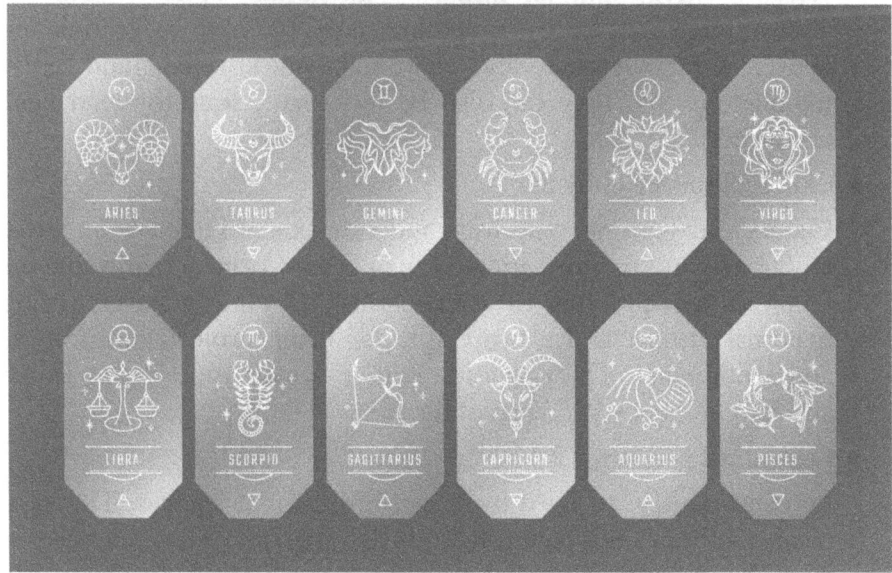

The sun signs.[13]

- **Aries (March 21 - April 19)**

    Being the first sign of the zodiac, Aries people are born pioneers - adventurous, courageous, and always eager to make a way for themselves. They have an independent spirit and a need to be first, to be the best, and to lead the charge. Aries suns are impulsive, energetic, and confident. They are not afraid to take risks and meet their problems head-on. Unfortunately, they can also be impatient, hot-headed, and quick to anger if they don't get their way.

- **Taurus (April 20 - May 20)**

    Taurus sun signs are known for their stability, practicality, and love for creature comforts. They are sensual, down-to-earth people who find joy in life's simple pleasures – good food, art, and comfortable surroundings. They're quite hardheaded, though, and dislike change the minute it interferes with their routine. They can be indulgent, possessive, and resistant to leaving their comfort zones.

- **Gemini (May 21 - June 20)**

    Gemini suns are the social butterflies of the zodiac – curious, communicative, and forever adaptable. They have a youthful, versatile energy and an insatiable intellectual appetite. They're always ready to learn something new or have a stimulating conversation. Geminis are charming, quick-witted, and great multitaskers, but they can also be indecisive, scatterbrained, and two-faced.

- **Cancer (June 21 - July 22)**

    Cancer sun signs are nurturers and caretakers. They are intuitive, emotional, and security-oriented people who place a high value on family, home, and their closest relationships. Cancers have a strong maternal instinct and a propensity for being protective, sensitive, and sentimental. The downside is they can be moody and clingy and have difficulty letting go of the past.

- **Leo (July 23 - August 22)**

    Leo sun signs were born to be performers and leaders. They are regal, confident, and have a flair for the dramatic. They want all the spotlight and admiration but are quite generous and charismatic. If you have a problem with a Leo, it's likely because you've seen them be arrogant, demanding, and easily offended if they don't receive the attention and respect they feel they deserve.

- **Virgo (August 23 - September 22)**

    The methodical perfectionism of this sun sign is a blessing and a curse. They have a good eye for detail, a practical, analytical disposition, and a compelling need to do things for people. Virgos are hardworking, conscientious, and good at problem-solving. Still, they are too critical, fussy, and anxious when things aren't going according to plan.

- **Libra (September 23 - October 22)**

    Libra suns are diplomats and peacemakers. They are charming, graceful, and elegant people who will do almost anything for balance and justice. Libras are skilled negotiators, mediators, and social butterflies. However, they can be indecisive, people-pleasing, and avoidant.

- **Scorpio (October 23 - November 21)**

    There is no sign as intense, mysterious, and passionate as Scorpio. They have a magnetic, penetrating aura about them and are very curious about anything hidden or considered taboo. They are brave, loyal, and resourceful but can be possessive and vengeful, with many trust issues.

- **Sagittarius (November 22 - December 21)**

    Sagittarius suns are always where the fun is. They love a good time like nobody else. They have a boundless curiosity about the world, a philosophical, optimistic outlook, and always want to know more. They are jovial, honest, and energetic people but can be reckless, impatient, and noncommittal.

- **Capricorn (December 22 - January 19)**

    Capricorn suns are ambitious, disciplined, and pragmatic. Some would say they are the opposite of Sagittarius. They want nothing more than to achieve their goals and come off as mature and very responsible. A Capricorn is stable and will never let you down, but you may find them too serious, pessimistic, and unable to relax.

- **Aquarius (January 20 - February 18)**

    Aquarius sun signs are not hard to recognize. They are unconventional visionaries and intellectual rebels. They are progressive, humanitarian, and would love nothing more than to challenge the status quo. Aquarius suns are independent, objective, and usually ahead of their time, but they can be aloof, detached, and emotionally disconnected.

- **Pisces (February 19 - March 20)**

    It has been said that Pisces suns have a bit of all the zodiac signs in them. They are the mystics and the dreamers. Their sensitivity, intuition, and empathy are their best and worst qualities. Of all the zodiac signs, they have the strongest connection to the spirit world. Pisceans are imaginative and romantic but can be idealistic, escapist, and unable to set boundaries.

Moon Sign

The moon always comes second to the sun. It is quiet in the backseat, and happy to be there. Although it doesn't demand the spotlight, that does not mean it isn't equally important. In astrology, the sun represents your outward personality and the face everyone sees, but the moon is what you hide beneath. It represents your emotions, your subconscious, and your base instincts - the *you* the world doesn't get to see.

Your moon sign hints at how you process feelings, what you define as safe, and how you connect to your intuition. The closest people to you may get to see this side of you, but generally, it is private. It is the WHY behind the WHAT.

Here's what your moon sign says about you:

- **Aries moon:** People with an Aries moon have very active, energetic emotions. They feel things intensely and react quickly. Their moods change suddenly, and they aren't afraid to boldly express their feelings, even if it's impulsive. They wear their hearts on their sleeves.
- **Taurus moon:** Taurus moon people are emotionally steady and grounded. They want comfort, security, and pleasure. They're emotionally reliable and nurturing but stubborn and hate when things change too quickly.
- **Gemini moon:** Those with a Gemini moon have quite changeable, curious emotions. You could say their emotions are butterflies fluttering from one feeling to the next. Their moods and thoughts flow as quickly as their thoughts. They like variety and mental stimulation, so their emotions lean toward being scattered or indecisive.
- **Cancer moon:** Cancer moons are sensitive and intuitive. They're deeply in touch with their feelings and are always searching for emotional closeness and home. They can be moody and clingy - but just as caring and nurturing.
- **Leo moon:** Leo moons have big, dramatic emotions. They look for attention, admiration, and validation when expressing themselves. Their feelings are fiery and proud - and a tad self-centered.

- **Virgo moon:** Virgo moon types approach their emotions practically, analytically, and meticulously. They can be especially critical of themselves and others emotionally because they want everything to be perfect. They worry a lot and get entangled in small emotional issues, but they are more discerning than any other zodiac.

- **Libra moon:** Libra moons want peace, balance, and social connection in their emotional lives. As charming and people-pleasing as they are, they're somewhat indecisive about their feelings because they'd rather have consensus and validation from people.

- **Scorpio moon:** Scorpio moons have emotions that are as intense and scary as the dark depths of the ocean. They're intuitive, mysterious, and secretive. They brood a lot, too.

- **Sagittarius moon:** Sagittarius moons are as free-spirited as they come. Emotionally, they want expansion, optimism, and new experiences. They are direct, restless, and philosophically inclined with their feelings.

- **Capricorn moon:** Capricorn moons handle their emotions with discipline, responsibility, and practicality. Anyone can see that they are emotionally reserved, ambitious, and a little melancholic. Stability and structure are vital for them whenever emotions are involved.

- **Aquarius moon:** Aquarius moon types have a detached, independent emotional style. They prefer to observe rather than engage. Overt emotional expression doesn't come easily to these people, so they prefer to process feelings through the intellect. They are not sentimental and would rather do things for the greater good.

- **Pisces moon:** Pisces moons are empathetic and in touch with their subconscious. Their feelings can be fluid, compassionate, and maybe even psychic, but they might get lost in unrealistic daydreams from time to time.

Rising Sign

The rising sign, known as the Ascendant, is one of the most important elements in a person's birth chart. It is the star sign that was rising on the eastern horizon at birth. Your rising sign is a tint on your worldview and your initial response to your circumstances. It's the first impression you make on people and the energy you radiate. Unlike your Sun sign, which is your identity, your Ascendant is your external self – your style, mannerisms, and habits. It is how your soul has chosen to interface with the physical world in this lifetime. It's the portal through which your essence manifests in human form.

What is your rising sign?

- **Aries ascendant:** They have a strong competitive streak that appears without them realizing it. They may inadvertently take over conversations or push their agenda, not understanding why everyone else doesn't match their bold, impatient energy.
- **Taurus ascendant:** Taurus ascendants appreciate the finer things in life. They love to indulge their senses, which is good until they become too attached to their material possessions.
- **Gemini ascendant:** Geminis are too curious. It is hard work for them to focus on one thing for too long before moving on to the next shiny idea. Hence, they are versatile but also hyperactive and inattentive.
- **Cancer ascendant:** Cancer ascendants pick up on the unspoken feelings and energies of people, whether they want to or not. They smother the people they care about.
- **Leo ascendant:** Leos are outgoing and confident, but they can occasionally come off as arrogant or showmanship.
- **Virgo ascendant:** Perfectionists to their core, Virgos as ascendants can be critical of themselves and everyone around them. They may worry about minor details, especially when they have too many options.
- **Libra ascendant:** Libra ascendants hate conflict and will go to great lengths to avoid it, even if it means compromising their values or opinions.

- **Scorpio ascendant:** Scorpio ascendants are private. The people closest to them know this about them and have made their peace with it. Scorpios will hold a grudge or get revenge if they feel they've been wronged.
- **Sagittarius ascendant:** As freedom-loving as they are, they can be a bit tactless or insensitive when expressing their bold opinions. Relationships or long-term plans might make them feel trapped.
- **Capricorn ascendant:** Driven and ambitious, Capricorn ascendants might seem aloof or cold. They don't know how to let their guard down. Their professional and social image matters more than anything.
- **Aquarius ascendant:** Aquarius ascendants could seem detached or dispassionate. They're not. They would sooner rationalize their emotions than fully feel and express them.
- **Pisces ascendant:** They feel everything all the time as intensely as possible. They don't believe they need boundaries, but they do.

Planetary Placements

The sun and moon aren't the only celestial bodies in your birth chart. Everybody knows their sun and star sign, few people know their moon sign and even fewer people know their other planetary placements. Every celestial body in the solar system is always in a zodiac sign. Your birth chart shows the precise zodiac sign all the planets were in when you were born.

Not counting the sun and moon, they've already been covered. There are nine planets in the solar system, each with its own energies and characteristics. The positions of these planets at your birth weren't random; they were intentionally chosen and stipulated in your soul contract. You must first understand each planet's energy to understand why.

Each planet has its own energy.[18]

Mercury

Mercury, the closest planet to the sun, is the planet that rules communication, intellect, and how you process information. As the messenger of the gods in Greek mythology, this planet governs your daily routines, problem-solving skills, and even how funny you are. Your Mercury sign influences how you express yourself, verbally and in writing. People with multiple Mercury placements usually have a sharp wit, lively curiosity, and talent for anything logic and analysis.

Venus

This planet is in charge of relationships, self-worth, and appreciation for the finer things. Venus is the Roman version of the Greek goddess Aphrodite, who is the embodiment of love, beauty, and pleasure. A Venus placement influences your approach to romantic partnerships, what you find aesthetically pleasing, and, in part, your financial tendencies. For example, Venus in Libra. To them, diplomacy and compromise matter most in their relationships, while a Venus in Taurus might be more into sensual indulgences and material things. Your Venus sign could help you understand your love language – how you prefer to receive love.

Mars

Mars represents physical energy, your drive, and your capacity for action. With links to the Greek god of war, Ares, your Mars sign shows how you prefer to assert yourself, how you channel your sexual energy and the physical activities that strengthen you, not drain you. A strong Mars placement means intensity, a competitive spirit, and instinctive leadership. For example, a person with Mars in Cancer might enjoy workout routines with a mind-body connection, while a Mars in Gemini might prefer the variety and mental stimulation of high-intensity interval training.

Jupiter

Jupiter is the largest planet in the solar system – the planet of luck, growth, and expansion. It has ties to the Greek god Zeus, ruler of the sky, grandeur, and abundance. Your Jupiter sign can show you the areas where you have the highest chances of experiencing good fortune and personal growth. Multiple Jupiter placements come with a natural joie de vivre and a belief in possibility.

Saturn

Saturn is called the taskmaster. This planet rules over discipline, structure, and the lessons you must learn to grow and mature. Your Saturn sign shows you where you might run into problems and limitations and where you'll need hard work and persistence. Saturn placements are serious, responsible, and firmly committed to their goals. For example, a Saturn in Aries might be impulsive and need to learn patience. In contrast, a Saturn in Libra desperately needs balance and compromise in their relationships.

Uranus

Uranus is the go-to for innovation, eccentricity, and freedom because of its association with the Greek god Ouranos, the original ruler of the sky and the embodiment of rebellion. Your Uranus sign could point you to your talents and your readiness to defy the natural order. Multiple Uranus placements normally have a pioneering spirit. They love originality and nonconformity.

Neptune

Neptune is the planet linked to the subconscious, spirituality, and the blurred boundaries between reality and fantasy. It has links to the Greek god Poseidon, ruler of the seas, lending to its mystery and the unknown. Your Neptune placements determine your intuition, your creative inclinations, and your penchant for escapism. Strong Neptune placements are highly sensitive and fascinated with the metaphysical. Neptune in Pisces is considered a strong placement because Pisces is already ruled by Neptune. So, this person will feel a stronger connection to the mystical than a Neptune in Virgo.

Pluto

Pluto is the planet with the strongest links to the human experience. It is connected to the Greek god Hades, the god of the underworld. Your Pluto placements show the parts of your life that require the most personal growth, where you need to release old patterns and transform. People with strong Pluto placements have an intensity about them. They are passionate and willing to march into the darkest regions of their psyche if needed.

The Twelve Houses of Astrology

The 12 houses in astrology represent the different spheres or areas of human life. They follow the developmental journey your soul takes, from the initial spark that separates your identity (1st house) to the inevitable dissolution back into the collective (12th house). The houses are not "energies" like the zodiac or planets. They are the fields or domains where those energies are most likely expressed. The houses are the WHERE, and the planets and zodiac are the WHAT. Here's a quick tour through the 12 houses:

There are 12 houses in astrology.[14]

- **1st House:** This is the house of the self – your personality, physical appearance, self-image, and how you initiate action. Energies here have a strong influence on your identity and first impressions.
- **2nd House:** This house is in charge of your resources, values, and self-worth. It deals with your relationship to money, possessions, and your hidden talents. Energies here influence how you earn, save, and spend.
- **3rd House:** Communication, information, transportation, and your immediate environment are the domain of the 3rd house. It includes siblings, neighbors, short journeys, early education, and the workings of your lower, analytical mind.
- **4th House:** Home, family, foundations, and the emotional roots that anchor you are represented by the 4th house. Energies here influence your domestic life, parental relationships, and personal security.
- **5th House:** This is the house of self-expression, pleasure, and the heart. It rules romance, creativity, children, hobbies, and risk-taking. Energies here spark joy, fun, and authentic self-display.
- **6th House:** Daily work, routine, service, and physical health fall under the 6th house. Energies here influence your work ethic, habits, and how you manage mundane responsibilities.
- **7th House:** Partnerships, one-on-one relationships, love affairs, etc., come into focus in the 7th house, including marriage, business collaborations, and open enemies. Energies here affect how you relate and cooperate with people.
- **8th House:** The 8th house rules over shared resources, sexuality, death, and transformation, including your partner's money, inheritances, taxes, and the psyche. Energies here illuminate your extent for intimacy and regeneration.
- **9th House:** This house rules higher learning, philosophy, religion, travel, and mental expansion. Energies here influence your quest for meaning, moral beliefs, and experiences that transcend your mindset.

- **10th House:** Status, achievement, and public reputation manifest in the 10th house. It represents your career path, social standing, and your role in the larger community. Energies here influence your ambitions and public persona.
- **11th House:** Friendships, group involvements, humanitarian concerns, and long-term goals manifest in the 11th house. Energies here influence your social consciousness.
- **12th House:** The final house governs the subconscious mind, self-undoing, confinement, and spiritual transcendence. Energies here determine your shadows, karmic baggage, and mystical and intuitive powers.

Astrology and Soul Contracts

The interpretation of pre-birth agreements through astrology is a complicated and subjective process. However, in the astrological community, special planetary alignments point to pre-agreements you made before incarnation. These alignments are:

- **Saturn Returns:** Every 27 to 30 years, Saturn returns to the same position it held when you were born. This return is a performance review, where the universe demands that you face the music and take a long, brutal look at the choices you've made and the responsibilities you've taken on. It's a time for reckoning, a period where you're asked to confront your fears and limitations and step into your power. As expected, many people aren't ecstatic about this because there will be issues that can't be ignored – crises that will force you to grow up. However, there's nothing to be afraid of. Saturn's return is your chance to shed the old skin and become the person you're truly meant to be. It's a time to honor the soul-level commitments you made and gain the wisdom that comes from facing your fears.
- **North Node and South Node:** The North and South nodes are points in your astrological birth chart representing where you're headed (North node) and where you've been (South node). The South node represents your past lives, the talents you incarnated with, and comfortable behavioral patterns. It's a well-worn path that feels familiar to you. The energies in your South

node show the qualities and skills you've developed over many lifetimes. While they can be a bonus in this lifetime, they can become crutches or limitations if you get stuck in them. The South node is your comfort zone and the habits that keep you from growing. Alternatively, the North node points to your soul's destiny and the areas where you're meant to stretch and evolve. The energies in your North node show you the qualities and life experiences you agreed to develop if you hope to fulfill your life purpose in this lifetime. They are there to push you out of your comfort zone.

- **Chiron:** Chiron was a centaur in Greek mythology - and a healer. Ironically, he also carried two painful wounds that could never fully heal: one *psychological* and the other *physical*. This contradiction - being a healer with an unhealed wound - is the essence of Chiron's astrological symbolism. Chiron's placement reveals the areas where you have the potential to become a wounded healer, where your pain can become the source of your greatest gifts. Working with this energy is not for the weak because it requires facing your wounds, feeling the full depth of your pain, and resisting the temptation to numb yourself. Chiron's energy teaches you to acknowledge your imperfections and to love yourself, flaws and all.

Planetary Alignments and What They Mean

Contrary to what you might think, planets and their influences are not separate and compartmentalized. Their energies affect the collective consciousness. These collective shifts are strongest during transits, retrogrades, and eclipses.

Transits

A transit is when a planet moves from one point in the sky to another. These movements are unavoidable, and as the planet moves, it passes through particular points in your birth chart. These pit stops always come bearing gifts for you and the collective. For example, Jupiter could be transiting over your 10th house, your career house. During this transit, you may notice expansion, new possibilities, or growth in your work life. Jupiter's energy (luck, abundance, and optimism) activates and influences your career as it passes over it.

Collective transits happen when a planet moves into a new zodiac sign, not only a point in your birth chart. Everyone is affected because its energy shifts the collective consciousness and experiences. For example, when Saturn enters Capricorn, generally, there is a greater emphasis on structure, responsibility, and the need for sustainable long-term solutions. Businesses and governments may tighten their belts, and people feel pressured to get serious about their goals and commitments. Or when disruptive Uranus transits into Aquarius, there's social change, technological advancements, innovation, and independence. If you're paying attention, you'll notice major cultural, political, or scientific breakthroughs during these transits.

Transits are not spontaneous; they can be predicted with near-perfect accuracy, so anyone can prepare for and harness these energies' influences when they happen.

Retrogrades

When a planet appears to be moving backward in the sky, this is called retrograde, and it happens regularly for all the planets. The most popular one is Mercury retrograde. During these 3 to 4-week periods a few times a year, communications, technology, and travel can get weird. Emails get lost, your computer crashes, your flight gets delayed, among other things. Mercury retrograde is a time to slow down, be extra mindful, and avoid making major decisions if possible.

Venus retrograde is another popular one that happens every 1.5 years or so. When the planet of love, beauty, and values seems to move backward, it's time to reassess your relationships, artistic projects, and what truly matters to you. Old flames may return, or you may need to renegotiate the terms of a current relationship.

The outer planets – Jupiter, Saturn, Uranus, Neptune, and Pluto, also have retrogrades that last for months. These longer retrogrades are an invitation to go inward and re-evaluate the big-picture themes and structures in your life. For example, a Saturn retrograde wants you to take a hard look at your responsibilities and commitments. Retrogrades, as frustrating as they are, are not punishment. They are for reflection and course correction. Everyone is better off using these energies to review, rework, and revise.

Eclipses

Spiritually, eclipses signal the end of one chapter and the beginning of another. A solar eclipse, when the moon passes between the sun and the Earth, can bring sudden changes like the end of a relationship or a new beginning. It is a very uncertain time, but this disruption is necessary to clear the way for positive transformation. Lunar eclipses, when the Earth passes between the sun and moon, are more associated with emotional awareness, intuition, and release. Secrets will come to the surface, or you may feel the need to let go of what no longer serves you. An eclipse interrupts the normal rhythms of the sun and moon, causing a cosmic reset. It is asking you to let go and trust the process. Trust that what's ahead is always better than what you leave behind.

What Is Your North Node?

North Node	Meaning
Aries	You're here to learn to be brave, to take the lead, to stand up for yourself, and to put your needs first.
Taurus	Your destiny is to find joy in the physical world and to appreciate beauty, comfort, and worldly pleasures.
Gemini	Your purpose is to be a curious, adaptable learner. You're here to experience new things, communicate better, and see things from many perspectives.
Cancer	Your destiny involves developing your emotional intelligence. You're here to create a safe, supportive home and care for the people in your life.
Leo	You're here to shine, find joy in self-expression, and lead confidently.
Virgo	Your destiny is to perfect your skills, pay attention to details, and serve others.

North Node	Meaning
Libra	You're here to learn to compromise and bring people together.
Scorpio	Your destiny involves the mysteries of life, death, and rebirth, as well as facing your fears.
Sagittarius	You're here to be a truth-seeker, visionary, and free spirit.
Capricorn	Your destiny is to develop discipline, responsibility, and practical mastery of the material world.
Aquarius	Your purpose is to be an innovative, humanitarian, and unconventional thinker. You're here to contribute to the greater good.
Pisces	Your destiny involves compassion, spirituality, and a connection to the universal flow. You're here to transcend the ego, surrender to your intuition, and serve as a healer or mystic.

Chapter 5: Exploring the Akashic Records to Find Your Mission

An infinite mega library containing the complete record of every soul's journey through time and space seems suspiciously unrealistic, but the idea is not as far-fetched as logic would claim. This library is not fiction. It is called the Akashic records. The Akashic records are a massive catalog comprising the past, present, and future of all beings, events, thoughts, and emotions that have or will ever exist.

The Akashic Records are like a vast library that holds the imprint of the soul's experiences.[15]

The word *"Akasha"* originates from the ancient Sanskrit language, meaning *"aether," "primary substance,"* or *"source of all that exists."* The Akashic records are encoded within this fundamental, primordial substance that runs through the entire universe. Like how the ocean holds the history and movement of every wave, current, and living sea creature, the Akashic records hold the complete energetic imprint of every soul's experiences, thoughts, and actions.

There are no known coordinates to this library. It is not located in a physical place but instead exists as a non-physical plane – a multi-dimensional database. Many believe that the Akashic records can only be accessed through altered states of consciousness, like in deep meditation, channeling, or working with a professional Akashic records reader.

Akashic records shape or form is evident in many religious and philosophical traditions worldwide. In Hinduism and Buddhism, the Akashic records are a basal component of the universe. The ancient Egyptians spoke of the Hall of Records, a hidden chamber underneath the Sphinx that contained the secrets of human civilization. In Judeo-Christian traditions, the Book of Life mentioned in the Bible is sometimes interpreted as a reference to the Akashic records.

According to Hindu cosmology, the universe is not a cluster of disparate and independent entities. It is an infinite integrated system governed by the principles of Brahman, the supreme, all-encompassing reality. The Akashic records are the manifestation of Brahman's eternal, all-pervading consciousness to Hindus. The Akashic records are not only a passive information bank but an active, living entity and a conduit for the exchange of energy, wisdom, and spiritual understanding. Every thought, action, and experience that has or will ever occur is recorded and stored within this intelligent, interconnected network.

The Hindus believe that access to the Akashic records is not limited to a select few but is everyone's birthright. However, the depth and clarity of your connection to this sacred place rests on your spiritual development, intuition, and receptivity to the cosmic energies that flow through everything. This library is essential to the Hindu concept of karma because it contains a detailed record of your past lives, including the actions, thoughts, and experiences that led to your existence. Access to this library means that you can finally understand your karmic patterns and the lessons you have yet to learn on your spiritual journey.

Akashic Records and Your Soul Contract

Since the Akashic records hold every piece of information on your soul's evolution, then the details of your soul contract are somewhere in that gigantic archive. You could go a step further and say that soul contracts are drafted using the information from this library. For the most part, it functions like a regular public library, except instead of books, you can borrow the complete energetic history and future potentials of every incarnation you've had. So, it makes sense that when your soul contract was being created, you "borrowed" the relevant files containing all the necessary details about your soul's past.

Fortunately, these records aren't only accessible in nonphysical form. Humans can and have reached into these metaphysical archives to retrieve information about their soul's journey. The information within the Akashic records is objective and impartial, reflecting nothing but the truth about a person's soul journey. It's not filtered through anyone's opinions or agendas. It's the pure, unvarnished truth about your soul's experiences. So, you wouldn't have to worry about anyone's preconceptions or judgments distorting your discoveries.

The Akashic records sound like a place where anyone, regardless of race, gender, or religion, would want to visit. Can you imagine all the information it contains about you and the *"you's"* that ever existed? Were you rich in your previous life? Were you a man or a woman? Did you fall in love? Were you a queen? How many former lives have you had? What was your first life? What did you look like? Who wouldn't want to know?

This is the backstage pass of all backstage passes. However, an Akashic reading should be about more than satisfying your curiosity about the past. Somewhere in those records is the information to keep your present-day choices and actions in alignment with your soul's highest good. You will understand why certain things happened the way they did and why you had to go through your experiences.

Clarity and self-discovery of this magnitude may not be as easy as you think. What you learn might be uncomfortable or painful to face. You may find past life traumas, unhealed wounds, or crippling terrors that have been silently influencing your reality. Are you brave enough to find out? Will you run away from your shadow? Are you ready to take responsibility for your life, or do you want to forever be a victim of circumstance?

How to Access the Akashic Records

The Akashic records are open to everyone. It does not discriminate, is not exclusive, and it does not judge. The only requirements are intention, respect, and receptiveness.

There is more than one way to connect with this library. You can use:

Guided Meditations and Visualizations

This is the most common technique for accessing the Akashic records. Guided meditations put you in a relaxed state. Your conscious mind quiets and your intuition becomes more receptive to energetic downloads.

During a guided meditation, you might be led through a sacred space in your mind's eye. This could be a library, hallway, or field. As you connect more with this imaginary place and the images become clearer, you might receive downloads - information, wisdom, or guidance - directly from Akasha.

The physical world is an illusion, a distorted reflection of higher dimensions. The mind has enough power to transcend the physical limitations of its earthly vessel temporarily. It's all about intention. With the right spiritual practices, the mind can do almost anything, including bridge the gap between the physical and the ethereal, where the Akashic records are found.

Prayer and Intention

Another tried and true way to reach the Akashic records is through prayer and intention. Setting a clear intention to connect with the records sends a request to the universe. It invokes help and direction from the Akashic guides.

Prayer can take many forms. You can say a few genuine words or perform more structured invocations. Some people have used affirmations, such as "I now open myself to the wisdom of the Akashic records" or "I ask the Akashic guides to share their knowledge with me." The exact wording is not as important as the sincerity and devotion you bring to the practice.

Akashic Reading

If you can't access your Akashic records on your own, you can hire a professional Akashic reader to be the bridge between you and this space. An Akashic reader has mastered the skills to consciously access the

Akashic records. They have undergone extensive training and spiritual development to hone their intuition and learn the protocols for respectfully and safely entering the Akashic space. Through meditation, energy work, pendulums, tarot, and other metaphysical means, they can channel information, messages, and wisdom relevant to your life's purpose, lessons, and relationships.

There's no such thing as a "wrong" question during an Akashic reading unless you try to access someone else's records. You're not allowed. Only you can access your records – and only with your explicit permission. Your reading might not make sense to you right away, but go with it, trust your intuition, and use your discernment. Ultimately, an Akashic reading gives clarity. It does not confuse you, so ask as many questions as you want. They are your records, and you are entitled to their wisdom.

Journaling and Inquiry

Journaling can also grant you access to the Akashic records. It sounds too simple, doesn't it? Sometimes, it can be. You'll need a book to write down your questions or areas you would like to investigate. This creates a tangible focal point for the Akashic guides to work with. Then, set an intention to connect with the library. Responses could come as intuitive realizations, feelings, or impressions. Write down whatever pops into your head, related or seemingly unrelated. Don't overthink anything, don't edit or censor yourself, just keep writing. Have patience and stay open-minded. The answers you want may not arrive in the form you expect, but they will come if you remain receptive and keep the communication lines open.

Dowsing

For this, it's better to use a pendulum, not dowsing rods, especially if you've never done it before. How it works is quite straightforward. Hold the pendulum, set your intention, and ask your question. In response, the pendulum will move. The movements' direction and pattern are answers, depending on what each movement means to you. You could set the intention that a forward swing means "yes," side-to-side means "no," and a circle means "I don't know." The only downside to this is that you can only receive yes or no answers from the Akashic records, meaning your questions must be *specific*.

Use a pendulum for dowsing.[16]

Channeling

Channeling is a controversial practice, and for good reason. As a channel, you're a living, breathing microphone for a multidimensional entity. You're trusting and surrendering your physical form to it. That's a big deal, and it is not a decision to be made lightly. You're essentially inviting a spiritual being, with its thoughts, personality, and agenda, to take over your body and speak through you. That's a lot of power to hand over, and it's understandable why some people feel uneasy about it.

Channeling has been around for centuries. Entire traditions are based around it and they all agree on one thing: it must be done with proper care, intention, and respect. You're not merely opening the door to some random entity – you're establishing a sacred connection with a higher intelligence that must be treated with the utmost respect. In this case, you're channeling the Akashic records, which requires great spiritual maturity. You must let go of your ego, your preconceptions, and your need for control. However, if you do it right, you get an experience that could be life-changing.

Benefits of Accessing the Akashic Records

- **Clarity on life's challenges and recurring patterns**

  Sometimes, clarity is all a person could ever want. Life is complicated enough without problems that refuse to go away. You're trying to plug a leak in a dam, only to have it spring up somewhere else. Wouldn't you want to know why you keep getting into the same unhealthy relationships? Why do you feel stuck in a career you only need to pay your bills? The answers are in your Akashic records. It could be that your patterns stretch back generations or lifetimes, or your purpose is connected to a talent you never took seriously. The Akashic records can give you understanding and direction to break free from the cycles that have kept you stuck.

- **Unresolved karma and how to heal them**

  The Akashic records can help you see into your past lives and the patterns that have carried over into your current incarnation. Karma is the universal law of cause and effect. So, if you have access to your past lives, you can understand the karmic patterns influencing your current life, especially unresolved karmas, which are the negative or unresolved incidents from past lives that will manifest until they are dealt with. For example, you may have participated in a betrayal or caused an abandonment wound in a past life. This unresolved karma could manifest in your life as failed relationships, trust issues, or commitment issues. When you understand this, you can begin to heal and release the emotional and energetic patterns that have driven these behaviors instead of going in circles for the rest of your life. When you heal karma, the effect of that singular act spreads through the collective consciousness and heals a part of humanity as a whole. Remember, everything is connected.

- **Understand your soul's purpose**

  Every person has a reason for incarnating, a contribution only they can make during their lifetime. The problem is that everyone forgets what it is as soon as they are born and spend their entire life figuring it out. Nobody starts a mystery novel from the middle because you need the first few chapters for context. You know there's a bigger story at play, but now, you have to piece it together as you read. The Akashic records can show you where you're supposed to go and the clues to get there. You don't have to force yourself into a predetermined path anymore because you'll know, with unwavering certainty, that you are here for a reason and that you matter in the grand scheme of things.

- **Strengthen your spiritual connection and intuition**

  The Akashic records hold the answers to all of life's questions - information, guidance, and wisdom far beyond your lived experiences and your logical mind. Your intuition is the key to everything. It is the thread that links you to everything else. Information travels up and down this thread with or without your awareness. It is one way to receive information or energetic downloads from within and outside the 3D. Your spiritual connection might get you access to the Akashic records, but it is your intuition that interprets and integrates the responses. Your intuition bridges the gap between the seen and the unseen, the known and the unknowable. It is the language your soul speaks and understands. Your job is to listen closely. When you even attempt to access the Akashic records, you listen to your intuition, and the more you listen, the better you become at recognizing it. Soon it becomes second nature, and you live in awareness of your connection to everything.

Access Your Soul's Records

1. You'll need to be in a comfortable position, seated or lying down.
2. Close your eyes and disconnect your awareness from the outside world.
3. Imagine your physical body is dissolving, becoming porous and permeable. Feel yourself becoming a glowing, energetic field, a swirling vortex of light and information.
4. Feel this field expanding until the boundaries between your consciousness and the universal consciousness dissolve. You are no longer a separate self. You are one with a unified field of pure potential.

5. As you surrender to this expansive awareness, you should pick up on discreet vibrations and frequencies. These energetic signatures are the Akashic records. See it in your mind's eye as a holographic matrix, inseparable from reality.
6. Imagine your energy field becoming a transmitter, a receiver, an encoder, and a decoder of this network. Your consciousness is now a tuning fork, attuned to the exact frequencies coming from this matrix.
7. See your energy field transform and take on a new geometric configuration. It is now an iridescent dodecahedron - the sacred, 12-sided shape that represents holistic interconnectedness and the highest consciousness. This crystalline structure is your portal, your interface with the Akashic space.
8. As you hold this visualization, imagine the dodecahedron spinning, vibrating, generating sound, and beaming with light.
9. Sink into this sensory experience and release expectations or preconceptions of what is happening. Your rational mind should be in reverent surrender so your intuition can take the lead.
10. Remain in this state until you notice what you intuitively know a library is materializing around you. It is not a physical space but a multidimensional intelligent matrix filled with information. The volumes on the shelves are not made of paper but of light, sound, and pure coded consciousness.
11. As you turn your attention to this library, notice that the "books" are opening and closing on their own, and you receive data snippets and cascades of symbolic meaning. Don't be afraid; remain calm and open.
12. If you have a particular question, hold that intention in your mind. Let your intuition guide you as you reach out and touch the pulsing, holographic archives.
13. Wait and pay attention; the information you seek will come to you in ways that transcend linear thinking.
14. You may receive a vision, a feeling, or a realization. You may hear whispers or feel an energetic imprint. Trust that Akasha is responding to you in the way it knows you will understand.

15. When you are done, show gratitude for the wisdom and understanding you've received.
16. Imagine your dodecahedral form receding and your consciousness gradually returning to your physical vessel.
17. Breathe in deeply and breathe out, then open your eyes.

Chapter 6: Connecting with Guides and Higher Beings for Clarity

Spirit guides as a concept is a highly misunderstood aspect of spirituality. Are they real? Are they not? On one side of the debate are those who believe in the existence of spirit guides - benevolent, non-physical entities assigned to support the soul's growth and mission. To them, spirit guides are real, tangible presences.

On the other side are the skeptics. Spirit guides are nothing more than a product of the human imagination - a comforting fantasy people create to cope with life and general misfortune. To them, non-physical entities guiding and assisting humanity are not supported by scientific evidence. They cannot be considered "real" in the conventional sense.

However, there's a third side. This group sees it as a personal, subjective experience that may or may not be for everyone. They'd rather approach the concept curiously and discernibly, not with blind belief or outright dismissal.

Connecting with your guides will bring you clarity.[17]

No matter what side you're on, the belief in a supernatural being that guides and protects humans has a place in every religion and twice as many traditions. There are guardian angels in Islam and Christianity, spirit animals in indigenous cultures, and ascended masters in Eastern philosophies. The Hindus have Ishta devata, there's an entire pantheon of gods and goddesses for the ancient Egyptians, Africans look to their ancestors, and Jews believe in maggids.

It is human nature to believe in something greater, something that can provide mentorship, protection, and a connection to the divine, especially where confusion, grief, or an existential crisis exists.

Spirit guides, to believers, are compassionate, immaterial entities that exist on a higher dimension and have a nuanced understanding of the human experience and the universal principles governing existence. They are manifestations of divine energy, acting as intermediaries between the physical and spiritual worlds. People have associated them with many archetypes or symbolic representations, like animals, ancestors, or angels, to better receive and understand their energies and messages.

Spirit guides provide clarity, direction, and wisdom when there is uncertainty, transition, or personal growth. They do this with intuitive nudges, synchronicities, and, sometimes, direct communication.

You are more than just your physical body. You have an eternal, non-physical form – the soul, which is connected to a higher intelligence or consciousness. The spirit guides are responsible for the soul. Their assistance cannot be forced or replicated. It happens organically in divine timing.

Types of Spirit Guides

Guardian Angels

Guardian angels are spiritual beings that, according to many beliefs, are entrusted to watch over and protect humans. For example, Christians believe in guardian angels because biblical passages imply that God appointed angels to watch over and guide people. Psalms 91:11 says, *"For he will command his angels concerning you to guard you in all your ways."*

In Islam, guardian angels are called *"Malak."* These angels record a person's deeds, good and bad, and intercede on their behalf with God. Surah Ar-Ra'd (13:11): *"For each [person] are successive [angels] before and behind him who protect him by the decree of Allah."* Every human has a guardian angel, a spirit being walking beside them, so they don't have to go through life alone. Believers say they have experienced their guardian angel's presence, especially in the form of unexpected help. For them, guardian angels are a source of strength and protection, even though you can't physically see them.

Ancestral Spirits

Cultures that don't see their dead as truly gone but as having transitioned to a different dimension as ancestral spirits. They maintain a connection to their dead for continuity and spiritual support despite death. You could see your ancestors in dreams or visions or feel them intuitively if your connection is strong enough. Many cultures venerate their ancestors. For example, in Africa and Asia, families keep altars or shrines dedicated to their ancestors. They say prayers, offer gifts, and perform rituals to honor their memory, ask for blessings, and draw upon the wisdom, protection, and spiritual energy of those who lived before.

Ascended Masters: Ascended Masters are people who, through their unrelenting dedication and spiritual evolution, have conquered the limitations of the physical world and reached enlightenment and mastery. Described as wise and compassionate beings who have become one with the divine, they work as guides and inspirations for those seeking spiritual understanding.

The title *"Ascended Master"* goes back to Theosophy and the I AM Movement. This movement's teachings maintain that Ascended Masters were once ordinary humans who transcended the human experience. They are no longer bound by the physical world – yet remain connected to it by choice for humanity's sake. Believers say the Ascended Masters work behind the scenes, sending love, healing, and guidance to those who are open to receiving them. They are living examples of what is possible when a person fully embraces their spiritual path. Some of the most popular Ascended Masters are Krishna, Jesus, Buddha, and Saint Germain.

Higher Self

The higher self is the true, pure version of you within the human vessel. It is the wiser, more expansive part of self that is connected to something greater than ego. As your normal, day-to-day consciousness worries about things like your physical needs and base desires, the higher self sees past this limited perspective. This part of you is already aligned with your highest values, your intuition, and your spirituality.

The higher self has been called the *"divine spark"* because it is not separate from the divine. It is the divine within you. It is a guiding light that knows what is true and good. You don't have to earn your higher self or search for it; it is already there, steadily conspiring with the universe for your highest good, even on days when it doesn't feel like it.

Animal Guides

Nobody said spirit guides have to be humanoid. Cultures as old as civilization have believed in animal guides. They believe everyone has one or more animals that are spiritually connected to them. These spirit animals have peculiar qualities, characteristics, and energies crucial to their person's path. Many cultures maintain that your spirit animal chooses you and then makes its presence known through signs, dreams, or synchronistic sightings of the physical animal in the real world.

There could be a bird you feel weirdly drawn to for no obvious reason, or you keep randomly seeing pictures of the same animal everywhere. These experiences are usually interpreted as your spirit animal trying to get your attention and inviting you to learn from its wisdom. Animal guides are quite protective of their person, watching over you and fighting for you.

Do Spirit Guides Interfere with Free Will?

Spirit guides are not enforcers. They do not control or manipulate you. Despite being free from the limitations that humans are bound by, they only guide, support, and lend perspectives that could help you. The decisions are always yours to make. They are every wise old mentor in the movies who gives the young hero invaluable advice and encouragement but never forces them to do anything. Your guides will share their suggestions and foresight with you, but they'll respect your autonomy to decide what feels right.

They are called guides for a reason. They are not here to live your life for you. If anything, their influence is subtle. They don't shout orders or unexpectedly take over your decision-making. They don't want you to blindly follow their instructions. They want you to develop your confidence and hone your discernment. They are most helpful when they inspire you to think for yourself, and that's all they want to do - help.

There may be times when your guides try to steer you in a direction that doesn't feel right. In these moments, you can go your own way and do whatever you want. They'll never punish or force you to comply. That's the beauty of the spirit guide-human relationship; it's a partnership built on mutual respect and trust.

Spirit guides can help you understand the lessons you are incarnated to learn. Assuming your lesson is about body dysmorphia, you could run into a total stranger at a coffee shop who, without knowing your story, tells you exactly what you need to hear, and the conversation starts a domino effect that changes your life. Your guides understand that life isn't only an intellectual exercise - your emotions and intuition are also involved. They see the big picture, the overarching themes, the lessons you've learned, and the greater purpose that underlies your most painful memories. They pick up on your heart's whispers that you are too afraid to hear and amplify them right back at you in a language they know you'll understand. Spirit guides are not omniscient; they don't have all the answers, but they do what they can to lead you away from pitfalls and in the right direction. You have free will, yet there is always more than one right direction.

Signs of Spirit Guide Communication

- **Gut Feelings**

Spirit guides love to communicate through intuitive nudges or gut feelings - those sudden hunches, not-so-random fleeting thoughts, or strong feelings that something is right or wrong, even if you can't logically explain why. Your guides send you messages by plugging into your subconscious to give advice, warnings, or clarity. These intuitive hits pop up out of nowhere without a rational explanation for where they came from or why. The messages are typically confirmations, realizations, or an urge to do something, avoid a situation, or pay closer attention to something.

Your relationship with your spirit guides depends on how well you can recognize, decipher, and trust what they tell you. Don't worry too much if you initially dismiss or doubt the messages, especially if your mind can't immediately make sense of them. In your defense, a bulk of it only makes sense in hindsight.

Some people need only one confirmation that they're not going crazy. Other people need as many as they can get, but none of that matters. What matters is the faith you have in your intuition, a faith that is hard-won and gives you the confidence to trust your spirit guides. The stronger your faith, the clearer the messages become, forming a positive feedback loop. Your intuition guides you, and your spirit guides reinforce your faith in your intuition by sending more easily recognizable signs. The signs have always been easily recognizable, but you have only started paying attention.

- **Synchronicities**

Another sign of a spirit guide's presence is uncanny, borderline supernatural coincidences or meaningful coincidences that are too perfect to be random. This could show up in your life as seeing the same number, symbol, or image in the most unrelated contexts, almost as if it is following you everywhere. It could also be a chance encounter with a person at just the right time or a piece of information showing up precisely when you need it.

These are called synchronicities. They aren't random happenstance - they're orchestrated by your guides to affirm your faith, to prepare you for something, or as an attempt to redirect you. There's so much happening in your life, so sometimes you need a little help or a reminder. Your guides know what to give you and when. Also, they have a sense of humor. These so-called coincidences could be their idea of a joke, a little wink from the other side. Hence, you must pay attention so that you get the joke and everyone has a good laugh.

Sometimes, it's your cue to stop, think, and figure out the message's meaning. What are they drawing your attention to? What is there to learn from this? What are you not seeing? You interpret synchronicities through presence and curiosity.

- **Messages Through Dreams or Meditation**

Your spirit guides have many ways to get in touch with you. One way is through your dreams and when you're in a meditative state. In the dream state, your guides can meet you directly to give you wisdom or guidance that feels crystal clear, even if the imagery is a tad symbolic or metaphorical. They could use anything from vivid symbolism and poetic metaphors to full-blown narratives that feel deserving of a sequel. It conveys their vital message. When you wake up, you're left with clarity, inspiration, or the desire to act based on your dream.

It's the same during meditation. Your guides can reveal themselves using sensations, thoughts, or epiphanies. The messages can be straightforward – a clear instruction or a vision. As long as you are receptive during meditation, you create an opening for your guides to meet you halfway.

- **Physical Sensations**

Spirit guides reach out through physical sensations. You could suddenly feel warm or get a tingling like electricity pulsating in a part of your body – mostly around the crown, third eye, heart, or solar plexus chakras. Some people say they have felt a literal touch, a breeze, or a presence beside them. You don't necessarily have to feel them; you can smell them, and your intuition knows what they mean. Physical cues are essential clues that your guides are near or actively trying to communicate.

Contacting Your Spirit Guides

Meditation

If you got a dollar for every time you were asked to meditate, how rich would you be? You hear it a lot, don't you? It's been mentioned a handful of times in this book already, but it is all they say it is. If you want to connect with your spirit guides, one of the best ways is meditation. Modern life has made the mind too loud and too busy. Life is so distracting that stillness seems far outside your comfort zone, but in stillness, you find the channels that connect you to your guides. The entire point of meditation is stillness and mindful awareness. When there is nothing but awareness, you can hear and feel them. They've been there the whole time; their messages just got lost in the noise. You need to relax and silence the noise, be present, breathe, and let them speak to you.

Meditation provides you with focus to reach a higher plane.[18]

Setting Intentions

This applies to anything you hope to succeed in. You plan before you execute. You think before you speak. You set goals and then achieve them. You set a clear intention, and then you contact your spirit guides. You could set an intention by saying, "I need help with so-and-so." Don't demand anything or try to force a response; that rarely works. Show genuine respect and gratitude, then listen. Your guides are more than happy to respond to your sincere invitation to communicate.

Automatic Writing

Write down questions or requests for your spirit guides on paper or in your notes app if you prefer to type. Take a few deep breaths, relax, and let the answers flow from your intuition. Whatever comes through, write it down. Don't worry about it making sense; you have plenty of time to figure that out. When you're done writing, leave it alone; don't look at it. Give your mind time to relax. If you have other things to do, go ahead. Return to your scribblings much later and see if the messages make sense then.

Divination

Spirit guides speak through oracle cards, pendulums, runes, and other symbolic tools. Divination is usually the go-to for multidimensional messages, but it is only one of many channels. Always center yourself and set your intention before you start so that your guides come in clearly to work with you. Trust your intuition; professional diviners do. They know the symbol's meanings they work with. However, they know it is more than that. You could be looking at the three of swords in a Tarot deck, and your message has nothing to do with the card's official meaning. Your message might be in the imagery, the colors, or an isolated symbol on the card in the deck. Your guides are trusting you to use your intuition to decipher the messages. They know you can, and deep down, you know it, too.

Ask Your Spirit Guides About Your Soul Mission

1. Go somewhere quiet and comfortable where you won't be disturbed.
2. Light a candle or incense to set the mood.
3. Breathe in deeply and breathe out three times. Feel your body relax.
4. Imagine walking through a beautiful garden. The air is fresh, and there's not a single worry on your mind.
5. As you continue down the path, quietly call on your spirit guides until you sense another presence with you.

6. Look ahead and see your spirit guide materializing from nothing. Their energy is so warm and loving that it instantly puts you at ease. This is a being you know you can trust with all your heart.
7. Walk to your guide and greet them. Thank them for coming.
8. Gently explain that you've come seeking advice about your soul's higher purpose. Ask your questions, all at once or one by one – it's up to you.
9. Walk with them as they telepathically share the answers to your questions. They will speak if they want or need to.
10. Concentrate with an open heart and trust that the information they share is divinely inspired. If you have follow-up questions, don't hesitate to ask them. They're here to give you as much clarity as possible.
11. When the exchange feels complete, you'll see a fork in the road. Thank them again, pick a path, any path, and walk. This time, alone.
12. Stay in this garden as long as you want until you are ready to rejoin the world.
13. Open your eyes.

Chapter 7: The Role of Karma and Past Lives

When a pebble is dropped into a still pond, the initial plop disturbs the water surface where it makes contact. Then, it ripples and expands from the center. These ripples are the karmic effects of the original drop.

Karma is the ripple effects of life.[19]

Karma is an ancient Eastern belief. It is a spiritual principle that relies on cause and effect. Karma teaches that your actions, thoughts, and intentions in this life can and will affect your future in this life or the next. Everything in the universe is interconnected, and your choices and behaviors, conscious or unconscious, cause a ripple in time extending beyond your immediate circumstances.

To understand karma, first understand that your destiny is in your hands. Every decision you make, every word you speak, and every action you execute sets in motion consequences that will shape the future, and not only yours. This single belief is why you must be mindful and intentional in everything you do; you are largely responsible for the direction and progression of many lives, especially yours.

Karma teaches compassion and empathy. Your actions have the power to change other people's lives for better or worse. If you understand this, you'll be more inclined to behave carefully and considerately. These changes, good or bad, don't happen immediately, but when they do happen, it's hard to tell what led to what. The laws in charge of this system are far above your pay grade.

Humans can't directly trace the actions that caused the effect. You think you know, but you don't. You're better off keeping your eye on all the dominoes in a massive, almost eternal arrangement, which is impossible. You might see how a tile knocks over the next one. Still, eventually, everything happens so fast and all at once that it's impossible to follow every domino as it falls. There are too many variables at play – the weight of the tiles, the angle they're placed, or the possibility of your 7-year-old sister dashing straight through your arrangement. However, even though you can't 100% predict or control every outcome, it doesn't mean the system is meaningless or that your arrangement doesn't matter. The "effect" to the "cause" could take years or lifetimes to come to fruition, but uncertainty shouldn't stop you from choosing compassion and kindness.

Karma Is Not Punishment or Reward

Karma has become a bad word. People hear it and immediately think there's a scorekeeper in the sky doling out rewards and punishments based on behavior. When you touch a hot stove, you get burned, don't you? Would you say that the stove punished you? Probably not. It's what you get when touching a hot stove. Would you call getting burned karma? Maybe, maybe not.

Karma is not an external force that plays judge, jury, and consequences. It is nothing but a feedback loop. It is a mirror that points your actions back at you. There is no life without choice – and every time you choose, it leads to one thing that leads to another and another, and somehow, the initial "plop" makes its way back to you. Your decision, good or bad, becomes the lesson you need to learn and grow.

Fixating on a scoring system, where virtuous deeds earn you points and misdeeds land you in the "bad karma" column, will cause you to miss the point. You'll miss the point by trying to rack up good karma points in a bid to avoid punishment. The point is in the details. When you think you're being punished, ask yourself, "What is this trying to teach me?" There are lessons to learn from even the positive fruits of your labor.

The most valuable lessons come wrapped in "good karma." When things are going your way, and you're on a winning streak, your first thought might be to pat yourself on the back and think you're doing it right. You are, but that's not all there is to it. The temptation is to be so content in the satisfaction from your achievements that your good karma becomes a validation from the universe. Everything is going well, so you think you have it all figured out, or you think your good fortune is proof of your superiority. Again, you're missing the point. Karma isn't a scoreboard.

Your successes can show you your blind spots, but if you get too attached to the results, you lose the lessons that came with them. Success exposes areas where you're stronger but also areas where there may still be room for growth. There is wisdom in humility, and remember that your wins can teach you something important about yourself.

Karma and Past Incarnations

Reincarnation and past lives are true for many people, even if they can't explain how or prove it. The déjà vu, the prophetic dreams, strange phobias, and uncharacteristic talents suggest that some souls have lived before and have accumulated knowledge and skills over many lifetimes.

You picked up skills or hobbies with surprising ease, as if you were born doing it. Also, you have fears or phobias in this life that you don't understand. For all you know, you could've been executed for expressing yourself in a past life, which has carried over into this lifetime. Talent and trauma are not bound by time and space.

Also, karma is not bound by time and space. The seeds you plant in one lifetime can sprout decades or even centuries later, and the seeds they produce can continue to spread and grow long after you're gone. Until you stop reincarnating, your current life will have trickles from your past incarnations. These trickles can be unconscious memories and imprints from another life to karma. Each incarnation comes with lessons. Some lessons you learned well, and you carry that wisdom with you. Others were missed or learned imperfectly, so you struggle with the same things, over and over, in different forms.

Past Life Regression

Past life regression is an exercise in hypnosis through which you directly access and consciously step into your previous incarnations. You get to see yourself in a different body and life. You get to live as they lived, feel what they felt, and see how you could've done better. Access to these past life lessons you missed – these karmas – frees you from the negative cycles and limiting beliefs that have stuck to you, like Velcro, because now you understand and know how to heal. A woman who was abused in a past life can finally understand and heal her commitment issues. A man haunted by memories of war and violence can finally discover the reason for his anger issues.

Looking far into the past sounds fun. Anyone would be curious. However, curiosity is only half of it. A past life regression could root out memories that are terrifying to confront, memories better left in another lifetime. Regression therapists believe this discomfort is a necessary part of healing, but that doesn't make it easier. Nobody will blame you for wanting to keep those skeletons firmly in the closet, locked away where they can't haunt you anymore. But the price you pay for avoidance is far greater than the temporary discomfort of regression. Past life regression is a chance to alchemize your painful pasts into self-actualization and enlightenment. Facing and integrating the unlearned lessons from your previous lives, you become a whole, authentic version of yourself in this life.

A trained hypnotherapist or regression therapist will guide you into and through the process using gentle, meditative prompts. First, you'll go into a dissociative state, then into a liminal space between waking and sleeping, where the subconscious becomes more accessible.

Once you're in this altered state, the therapist will invite you to recall impressions, sensations, and images from a past life, often starting with the moment of your death. The things that are exposed can be eerily vivid and detailed – the sights, sounds, and physical sensations from another time and place. People have vividly seen clothing, architecture, and family from their former lives. The emotions you'll experience can be as real and poignant as any you feel in your current incarnation.

You may be disoriented as you are transported to an entirely different era with a different identity and life experiences. The detail and authenticity can feel more like a memory than imagination. You could be looking through the eyes of a young peasant girl in medieval Europe or a Spartan on a battlefield. The visceral sensations – the scratches from rough fabric, wound stings, and exhaustion – can feel startlingly real, and these sensations come with emotions, positive and negative, such as joy, sorrow, fear, and anger. People have wept uncontrollably over a long-lost love or were shaken to their core in terror as they relived their death, but, like every spiritual experience, there's more.

The healer from your medieval past reincarnated as you, a nurse or midwife in this life, or the betrayal you suffered in another life could help you understand your trust issues and perhaps find peace. Every lifetime is another chance to integrate the lessons of the past and grow beyond them. Karma has led you to this life, where you have nothing but an opportunity to transmute your lessons into power.

Karma Is the Foundation of Your Soul Contract

A soul contract mirrors the soul's highest intentions, which are not fixed. Your contract is adapted as your soul passes through lifetimes, carrying lessons from the previous life to the next. Your karmic lessons determine the basis of your soul's contract in this lifetime because the soul is not bound to repeat its lessons forever. It wants to address and integrate the karmic debts it owes, so it drafts a contract and soul plan.

The commitments between your soul and other entities (other souls, spiritual guides, or divine forces) are affected by the karmic lessons your soul carries. These commitments are how your soul creates the opportunities and circumstances to heal, grow, and reach enlightenment. It is all stipulated in your contract. You agreed to let your best friend betray you so that you could clear your karma by learning to open your heart again. It was so painful that it almost broke you, but it was co-created with the highest intention to help you fulfill your destiny.

Not every painful experience is a karmic rebalancing, and not every karmic rebalancing is a painful experience. This goes back to free will. You don't have to honor your soul contract, and other souls don't have to honor the contract they made with you. It would be nice if everything went according to plan, but that doesn't always happen.

A soul might have incarnated with the agreement to help you when you turned 28, but when the time came, they turned you away at great cost to yourself. They may have had other things to deal with, or perhaps they had a change of heart. Or maybe the timing wasn't right, and the expected support never materialized. They may incur a karmic debt or not, but the pain you went through had nothing to do with you. Sometimes, life can hand you complications that have no deeper metaphysical meaning. Sickness and accidents can cause pain without a grand "reason" behind it. The same goes for joy. Blessings don't always have to be good karma or perfectly aligned. Life is spontaneous, and while your soul contract is the path to your destiny, you must find the balance between trusting in the bigger picture and acknowledging the randomness and uncertainty of the human experience.

Types of Karmic Patterns

- **Recurring types of relationships or conflicts**

The déjà vu you feel when you're in another toxic relationship or having the same old argument could make you wonder if your life is on repeat. You're clearly stuck reliving the same experiences. But why? People have always said that the lessons you don't learn will never leave you alone. The recurring themes in your life aren't coincidences. They are karmic. They are the lessons your soul is trying to work through in this lifetime. All your toxic exes might be your soul needing to learn that it is okay to put yourself first. If you keep having the same fights with different people who have nothing in common, maybe it's time to look in the mirror and stop making excuses for your behavior. Your karmic debt is not punishment. Without it, you may never learn, and you risk staying stuck in the past, one lifetime after another.

- **Unexplained fears, passions, or skills**

Fear hardly makes sense to those who haven't felt it. You've met people with fears that make zero sense to you and them. They can't explain why they are afraid of ants or why they hate the sound of metal on metal. They'll say they were born that way. Some people were born prodigies. They have skills that people go to school for years to learn. Nobody in their known lineage ever had this skill, so where did it come from? These are signs of karmic imprints from past lives. Your irrational fear of water could be because you drowned or almost drowned in many lifetimes. You've sung well since you were 10 because you spent lifetimes honing your talent. The patterns you carry into this life, karmic or not, are your soul's attempt at healing and integrating other parts of itself. You must understand these unexplainable things about yourself to see how they fit into the larger machine that is your destiny.

- **Strong connections with certain people or places**

There's nothing like when you meet someone for the first time, and it's like you've known them forever, or when you visit a place that feels strangely familiar, even if you've never been there before. These are the signs of a karmic bond. Karmic bonds are connections from past lives that are now resurfacing to be investigated and resolved. Instant soul recognition with a stranger could be a soul contract activation between you - an agreement you made long ago to come together and work through some unfinished business. The pull you feel to a strange place might be because you have something important to learn or do there. Karma is always working in your favor; your soul knows this, and there'll be less resistance if you know it, too.

Karma, Soul Contracts, and Free Will

With all this talk about soul contracts and karma, it's fair to think you're merely along for the ride, like the universe has a plan for you, and you can't do much about it. However, you couldn't be more wrong. You are the one in charge. You're the one with the power. Your free will is your power. If karma is the structure of a house and soul contracts are its building schematics detailing the layout and function, then free will is what you do in the house. It's the color of paint you choose, the furniture you buy, and where you place said furniture. It's how you make the house a home. It's like moving into a new apartment. The foundations and blueprints were laid out before you moved in, but you get to make it your own.

The same goes for your life. Only you can interpret the role you've been tasked to play. Only you can choose what you do with the opportunities you've been given, not karma and certainly not your soul contract. You're not a spectator in your life; you are a co-creator.

If you were "destined" to have toxic, codependent relationships in this life, your free will gives you the power to recognize it, do the shadow work, and choose healthier relationships. If your soul agreed to have a neglectful or abusive parent in this lifetime, that's the karma and soul contract you're working with. How do you respond to that? Whether or not you perpetuate the cycle or heal, grow, and break free is up to you.

Your free will is how you break cycles. It is how you understand your karma, do the healing, and create a different future, not only for yourself but for future generations. You don't choose all your life's circumstances, but you do get to choose your responses.

Ways to Clear Your Karma

Now that you know the universe isn't conspiring against you, how can you regain your power, clear your karma, and co-create your life:

- **Acts of kindness and compassion**

Sometimes, all it takes is to be kind, not performative, surface-level kindness, but the *real thing*. There's humanity in everyone you meet, even those who rub you up the wrong way. Treating people with kindness is the barest minimum anyone deserves. So, hold the door open for a stranger, say please and thank you, and help an old man cross the street. Also, be kind to animals. Take that wounded cat to the vet, feed the neighborhood dog, or free the squirrel caught in a net. Kindness should be given freely to every living thing, including you. Be kind to yourself, love yourself, appreciate the things you've done, and celebrate how far you've come. The more kindness you give to yourself, the more you have to give to others, and the more you will receive in return. A kind word can change someone's day or, better yet, their life.

- **Forgiveness**

One of the most powerful ways to reclaim your power and clear your karma is to forgive. Hard as it might be, there is no need to hold onto grievances, resentments, and mistakes – yours and those of others. It's too heavy to carry through an entire lifetime, much less two. Everyone is flawed and doing their best with what they know. Forgiveness doesn't mean it didn't hurt or they didn't do anything wrong. It means you choose to drop the dead weight of anger. You elect not to let the wrong that was done to you define you. This is a gift, even if they don't know it. It is a gift that you give to them and yourself. Forgive yourself as willingly as you forgive others. Let it go and make room for love, healing, and change.

- **Conscious choice aligned with love and growth:**

It's one thing to know what you must do and another to follow through. You see a boy getting bullied. You know it's wrong, but do you speak up or stay quiet? Everyone can see that your relationship is bleeding you dry. You see it, too. Will you walk away, or will you sacrifice yourself on the altar of love repeatedly? It takes guts to make conscious, loving, growth-oriented choices that go against the grain, the hard choices. It would be so much easier to stay quiet, keep your head down, and remain stuck in the soul-sucking situation because at least it's familiar, but where's the growth in that? When you choose love and growth over fear and complacency, the universe will return the favor. What you think you'll lose by choosing growth are the anchors keeping you from reaching your highest self. Your life story unfolds with every choice. So, what will it be?

- **Taking responsibility for your life**

You and everyone else have had your fair share of hardships and heartbreaks that felt completely out of your control. However, you are not always at the mercy of your circumstances. Victim mentality is more addictive than people realize. If you allow it, it'll keep you ensnared in the same karmic patterns you're so desperately trying to transcend. You may not like the hand you've been dealt, but it is your choice what you do with it. You give away a bit of your power every time you point the finger, make excuses, or let yourself off the hook. Face your shadow and ask yourself, "What part did I play in this?" "What can I do to make it better?" This is how you choose growth over victimhood and compassion over judgment. It is how you find the light in the dark.

Past Life Regression Exercise

1. Close your eyes. Breathe in through your nose and out from your mouth. Let the tension melt away one exhale at a time.
2. In your mind's eye, see a staircase in front of you. Not just any staircase but a beautiful, winding staircase. You're at the top of this staircase.
3. Make your way down.
4. With each step, feel yourself relaxing. Let reality fade into the background as you climb down the stairs.
5. You're at the bottom now, and there's a long, poorly lit tunnel a few feet ahead. Enter the tunnel.
6. You should see many doors lining the walls. Each door is a different color and energy. Which one is calling to you? Use your intuition.
7. Walk to it and place your hand on the handle. Turn the knob and push it open. This door will take you to a different lifetime. Enter when you are ready.
8. Look around. What do you see? What do you hear? What bodily sensations do you feel? What are you wearing? Try to get a feel of who you were. Where are you? Is there anyone around you?
9. Let the details and emotions come to you naturally. Don't worry about trying to figure it out. All you need to do is be present and observant. Breathe it all in, the air, the sounds, and the emotions from that time.
10. When you're ready to leave, imagine a portal behind you. It is the door you entered to get here. Make your way back into that tunnel and close the door.
11. Climb up the staircase, and when you get to the top, open your eyes.

Affirmations

Positive affirmations are statements you repeat to yourself for yourself. They can be just the things you need when you are ill, in a dysfunctional relationship, or working through unhealthy habits, which could be manifestations of karma. Your thoughts hold so much weight. They are powerful enough to untangle you from negative karmic cycles.

Repeat these affirmations daily for 21 days and see how much power truly exists in your mind:

- I release all energies, patterns, and beliefs that no longer serve my highest good.
- I am worthy of love and abundance.
- I am surrounded by divine light and protection always.
- I forgive myself.
- My mind is clear, calm, and open to receiving guidance from my higher self.
- I trust my journey and accept all my lessons gracefully.
- I am a powerful creator.
- My body is a temple, and I treat it with love, care, and respect.
- I am connected to the universe.
- I am grateful for the blessings in my life, past, present, and future.
- I release all fear and resistance. I am limitless.
- I am a magnet for miracles, synchronicities, and joy.
- I am divinely guided at all times.

Chapter 8: Creating Your Soul Plan

Your soul plan is alive. Not in the sense that it has a physical body or a beating heart, but alive in the energetic sense. It can be updated and renegotiated as you change and your priorities shift. It communicates with you through synchronicities, intuitions, and dreams. It is responsive to your actions, thoughts, and beliefs.

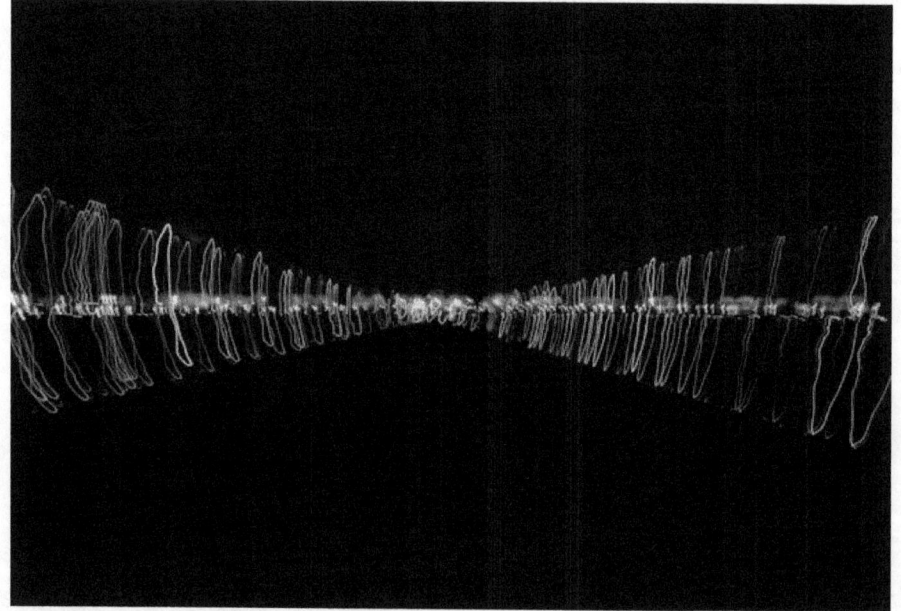

Your soul plan is already energetically alive.[30]

When you live in alignment with your highest good, your soul plan supports and amplifies the positive energies. However, when you do things that do not elevate your consciousness, your soul plan may offer you options to course-correct or to learn from the consequences of your choices. It doesn't only influence your life. It is the reason for your life.

Your pre-birth agreements are not alive in this way. They can also change, but they remain relatively the same. Your physical form is a pre-birth agreement, and so is your family lineage, your sensitivities and proclivities, your spirit guides, and your relationships. These meticulously chosen elements are based on your soul's frequency, psychic imprint, and karmic history.

Pre-birth agreements may be concluded before your birth, but your soul plan is never complete. It cannot be complete because it responds to you, and your choices dictate the route from incarnation to destiny. You and your higher self work together to direct your soul plan for your mortal life. You are responsible for how things unfold, not the other way around.

How to Shape Your Soul Plan

- **Soul Contracts**

The relationships in your life, intimate and casual, are not random. Your souls agreed to incarnate together in the same era, but why? What reason could you both possibly have for this? What is the purpose behind the people who enter and exit your world? These are the questions you should ask as the co-creator of your destiny. If you woke up with amnesia one day and your sister told you that you both saved $50,000 before you lost your memory, wouldn't you want to find out why? What were you saving for? When did you start saving? Where are the savings? You're not as curious about your pre-birth agreements because you don't know what to be curious about or if there's anything to be curious about. There is. Your souls chose to meet for a reason, and neither of you remembers the reason. So, half the fun is figuring it out. Here's a hint: you are here to expand your consciousness. What about your soul contract can help you achieve that? What lesson is this meant to teach you?

- **Numerology**

Numbers are energy. Your birth date is energy. The letters in your name are energy because they represent a number. You don't need to be a numerologist to know what the energy in a single digit says about your personality, life path, and destiny. You can do these calculations and follow the breadcrumbs your soul has left you to find your purpose.

- **Astrology**

Astrology is not only for horoscopes and fortune-telling. It offers much more than love compatibility readings. The planets exert as much influence over your life as the moon does over the ocean's tides. Natal charts are important, yes, but so are retrogrades and transits. These celestial patterns inch you closer to why you came to Earth. The skies are one of the few places with clues and assistance. Everything you see down here is a mirror of something up there.

- **Akashic Records:**

Stashed away in a library (larger than you have and will ever see) is a complete story of your soul's journey through time. Every incarnation, mistake, love story, and heartbreak is recorded with perfect accuracy in the Akashic records. It is not out of reach. Using meditation, your intuition, or working with an Akashic records reader, you can visit or call forth data from this place. There is much to learn from your previous incarnations. You have advice for your younger self, don't you? Well, what advice would you give to your next life if you could? Your answer is wisdom from only one lifetime. Imagine 50 or 1700 lifetimes. The information from these sacred records can help you make sense of your problems. It can reveal your soul's highest calling. The Akashic records contain all the answers – if you will only look.

- **Past Lives**

Your past lives are all the versions of you that incarnated for a mortal experience. Your soul is immortal and limitless, but some lessons can only be learned within the limits of a mortal life, especially a human one. The chances are, you've lived many lives before this one, and still lessons to be learned from them, or you won't need to reincarnate anymore. Figuring out the lessons is half the work, and too many people spend their entire lives not achieving them. Your past lives are a clue into the lessons you must still learn and the karma you must clear. Akashic records are a way to see into those lives. However, past life regression allows you to be in those lives. In these sessions, you get a front-row seat to life as another you in another time and place. You get to see what happened and how it could affect what is happening now.

- **Guidance from Higher Beings**

Your soul plan includes a group of higher beings that watch over you, guide, and help you. Human life is unpredictable. There are too many seen and unseen moving pieces. You may be able to maneuver the seen pieces, but what about the unseen? What about the forces beyond human comprehension? You're living a mortal life, and there is a limit to your capabilities. Beings from a higher place of consciousness don't have the same limitations, which is why you enlisted their help on your life journey. Some of these beings are always with you, protecting you and guiding your steps. Others are available to you, but only if you ask. Depending on your beliefs, you could have guardian angels, ancestors, animal guides, and many more. None of these beings, as powerful as they may be, can override your free will. So, once again, you are in charge of your life. They do what they can from the unseen world, but everything still hinges on your decisions. Meditation, journaling, and mindfulness are a few ways you can reach your spirit guides. Be open to their wisdom because they can see from much higher perspectives than you. You can co-create your soul plan, learn your lessons with them, and arrive at destiny's door already living in alignment with your highest self.

Steps to Co-create Your Soul Plan

Step 1: Reflect on Your Soul's Purpose

You'll never know what you are here to do if you never consider it. Self-reflection is the first step to understanding the meaning and lessons you're supposed to learn in this lifetime. It won't give you all the answers, but it is a solid start. Your soul knows the answers and whispers them to you constantly, except it's only loud enough when you're ready to hear them. When you're ready, you will ignore the external noise to find the internal whisper. If you're ever lost and you need clarity, ask your questions and then truly listen. You can't know yourself if you don't look at yourself. Step one to finding your purpose is getting to know yourself. What do you like? What is one thing guaranteed to make you smile? What values will you never compromise on? What do you think you do well? What is the hardest thing you've ever had to do? This is how you know the legacy you're meant to leave on the world. A curious mind will always find what they are searching for.

Step 2: Set Spiritual Intentions

Using what you learned from your self-reflection, set 4 or 5 intentions that intuitively feel right in your soul. These intentions should be themed in synchronicity with your spiritual mission.

Good examples are:

- Find ways to give back and be of service to my community
- Find healthy outlets for my difficult emotions
- Reconnect with the natural world and all living things
- Let go of my need to control everything
- Get closer to God and spirituality
- Speak the truth clearly and courageously

Your intentions will only work if they are yours. Your path is yours, and your intentions should be too. Nobody else can walk your journey for you, so it's better to set intentions that matter to you, not what you think you should want or what worked for someone else. The intentions you set today will be your light in the dark tomorrow.

Step 3: Identify Focus Areas

Focus areas include relationships, career, health, creativity, personal growth, or what feels important. Choose, at most, 3 focus areas to work on at a time. Other areas might need your attention, but these three take priority because they directly affect whether or not you live out your destiny. If learning boundaries and self-love are critical to reaching your destiny, a focus area could be self-care. You could set more intentions, do more self-reflection, or make more intentional changes in this area. The bulk of your time and attention will go into your focus areas as you work with your soul plan. Where is there a need for your attention and focus the most?

Step 4: Develop an Action Plan

Assuming you have your focus areas, next, you'll need three to five realistic actions that will move you toward your intentions.

All your actions should have three things:

1. They must be tangible. Anything too vague or open-ended won't give you clear steps to follow. Meditating more is more tangible than "being more spiritual."

2. They need to be measurable. Can you track the action's progress or not? How do you know when you've accomplished something? Meditating for 10 minutes every Thursday is much better than "meditating more."
3. They must be actionable. The steps you write down should be what you can actively do, not passive intentions. "Be more connected to nature" is passive. "Take a nature walk three times a week" is actionable.

Combined, these three elements – tangibility, measurability, and actionability – are your action plan.

Step 5: Stay Open to Guidance

Take as much help as you can get. Your mortal life is limited, even if you live to 300 years, which is a drop in the ocean compared to immortality. Your soul is immortal, but your human vessel isn't, so make the most of your time here. Your higher self and other spirit guides will send you cues, synchronicities, and opportunities that you won't see coming. Take the help. Keep an eye out for the signs; your intuition will know them when you see them. Stay open to redirections and trust that your higher self will guide you. Follow the breadcrumbs, not blindly, but follow them. Often, your job is to show up and decide – while the rest unfolds in divine timing. Trust the process; you are far from alone.

Exercise

Step 1:

Describe yourself in three sentences:

_____
_____
_____
_____

Which three values will you never compromise on:

_____
_____
_____
_____

If you could have a superpower, what would it be and why?

_____
_____
_____
_____
_____

What is your biggest flaw?

_____
_____
_____
_____
_____

What three bad habits do you have?

_____
_____
_____
_____
_____

Write down five things you are afraid of:

_____
_____
_____
_____
_____

Step 2:
Write down five intentions for this year:

_____
_____
_____
_____
_____

Step 3:
What areas of your life need your attention the most?

_____
_____
_____
_____
_____

Step 4:
What can you do to fulfill your intentions?
Intention 1:

_____
_____
_____
_____
_____

Intention 2:

_____
_____
_____
_____
_____

Intention 3:

_____
_____
_____
_____
_____

Intention 4:

_____
_____
_____
_____
_____

Intention 5:

_____
_____
_____
_____
_____

Step 5:
What higher beings do you look to for guidance?

_____
_____
_____
_____
_____

Tips for Living in Alignment with Your Soul Plan

- Begin your day with mindfulness, even for 5 minutes. Breathe and set an intention for how you want to show up that day.
- Write down 4 things you're grateful for at the end of every week.
- Schedule regular check-ins to review your intentions and action plan. Perhaps once every two weeks?
- Unplug from social media for at least 30 minutes every day.
- Move your body in ways that make you happy. Dance, do yoga, go for a run, do whatever brings you joy.
- Do something creative once every week.
- Review your calendar and schedule non-negotiable "me time." Protect this time fiercely.
- Ask yourself daily, "What's one small thing I can do today to move closer to my intentions?" Then do it.
- Keep a running list of synchronicities, signs, and intuitive messages you receive. This reinforces your trust in the process.
- Before bed, think about the highs and lows of your day. What did you learn? How can you apply this wisdom tomorrow?
- Look forward to surprise and spontaneity throughout your day. Connect with your inner child.

Conclusion

Nothing is a coincidence, not entirely. There are no isolated events in the universe. One thing has always led to another, and everyone is always where they should be. It may not be where you want to be, but that's why it is so beautifully precise. Give or take, there are eight billion people on the planet. So, eight billion soul contracts – and each is meticulously orchestrated by a greater, loving intelligence.

What about the sheer improbability of your life? From the trillions of potential sperm and egg combinations, you were the one that came to be. From the instant you were conceived, you have been guided by unseen forces that have led you to this exact moment in time. The friends you've made, the jobs you've had, the loves you've lost and found, and your body type was not a coincidence. Your soul chose this, and you, a physical embodiment of these choices, were beautifully crafted long before you were born. You are creativity made flesh.

Live your life in faith that everything is happening in perfect precision. Live in kindness because every energy you send into the universe through your choices is fed into the system to produce an effect mirroring the original choice. Live in awareness that you are a co-creator, a necessary addition to the collective consciousness. Live as powerfully as you are. There is no exact copy of you anywhere else. You matter, your choices matter, and you are here for a reason.

If you enjoyed this book, I'd greatly appreciate a review on Amazon because it helps me to create more books that people want. It would mean a lot to hear from you.

To leave a review:
1. Open your camera app.
2. Point your mobile device at the QR code.
3. The review page will appear in your web browser.

Thanks for your support!

Here's another book by Mari Silva that you might like

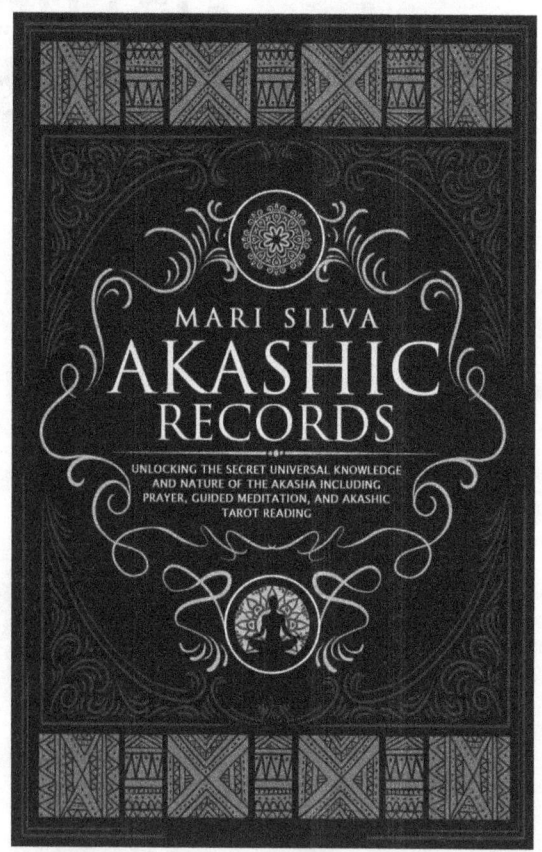

Your Free Gift
(only available for a limited time)

Thanks for getting this book! If you want to learn more about various spirituality topics, then join Mari Silva's community and get a free guided meditation MP3 for awakening your third eye. This guided meditation mp3 is designed to open and strengthen ones third eye so you can experience a higher state of consciousness. Simply visit the link below the image to get started.

https://spiritualityspot.com/meditation

Or, Scan the QR code!

References

Acharya Prashant. (2021). Karma. Penguin Enterprise.

Cayce, E. (2006). Reincarnation & karma. A.R.E. Press.

Decoz, H. (n.d.). Master Numbers in Numerology | World Numerology. Www.worldnumerology.com. https://www.worldnumerology.com/numerology-master-numbers/

DiMaggio, J. (2020). I Did It to Myself...Again! Balboa Press.

Jackson, D. (2020, August 3). Did Pythagoras invent numerology? AskAstrology. https://askastrology.com/numerology/did-pythagoras-invent-numerology/

Marlene, C. (2018, January 12). Prepare For Your Akashic Record Reading - Cheryl Marlene. Cheryl Marlene. https://www.cherylmarlene.com/prepare-for-akashic-record-reading/

Petrovic, J. (2023, August 17). Being Awakened. Being Awakened. https://www.beingawakened.com/past-life-regression/

Sloan, E. (2021). In Astrology, Each Planet Has Symbols and Meanings: Learn What They Are To Understand Your Birth Chart. Well+Good. https://www.wellandgood.com/astrology/meanings-of-planets-in-astrology

Team, T. N. (2010, February 15). The history of numerology. Numerologist.com. https://numerologist.com/numerology/the-history-of-numerology/

Tucker, J. B. (2021). Before. St. Martin's Essentials.

Wetzel, L. J. (2011). Akashic Records. Hot Pink Lotus POD.

Image Sources

1. Designed by Freepik. https://www.freepik.com/free-photo/top-view-hand-holding-love-letter_60249887.htm#fromView=search&page=3&position=10&uuid=ad80e677-dee6-4bda-aa37-ceb249bced5f&query=fantasy+contract
2. Photo by Justin Luebke on Unsplash https://unsplash.com/photos/person-in-yellow-coat-standing-on-top-of-hill-BkkVcWUgwEk
3. Rursus, CC BY-SA 3.0 <https://creativecommons.org/licenses/by-sa/3.0>, via Wikimedia Commons https://commons.wikimedia.org/wiki/File:Birth_chart.svg
4. Photo by Pixabay: https://www.pexels.com/photo/seven-white-closed-doors-277593/
5. Photo by Jean-Christophe André: https://www.pexels.com/photo/iceberg-2574997/
6. Designed by Pikisuperstar on Freepik. https://www.freepik.com/free-vector/modoern-people-doing-cultural-activities_9178339.htm#fromView=search&page=1&position=32&uuid=5f3a42e8-139f-4404-811a-21f67845f6ea&query=life
7. Photo by Pixabay: https://www.pexels.com/photo/group-of-people-on-street-260907/
8. Photo by Kevin Malik: https://www.pexels.com/photo/woman-sitting-on-rock-near-body-of-water-9032518/
9. Designed by Freepik. https://www.freepik.com/free-vector/hand-drawn-numerology-background_35706728.htm#fromView=search&page=1&position=0&uuid=d8ecd26f-151d-4fa9-ad64-1a1f0a17d308&query=numerology
10. File:Tree of life wk 02.svg: Cronholm144derivative work: נדב ס, CC BY-SA 3.0 <https://creativecommons.org/licenses/by-sa/3.0>, via Wikimedia Commons https://commons.wikimedia.org/wiki/File:Tree_of_life_He_02.svg
11. Photo by Marco Milanesi: https://www.pexels.com/photo/seven-sisters-constellation-15586141/

12 Designed by Pikisuperstar on Freepik. https://www.freepik.com/free-vector/gradient-zodiac-sign-collection_15056777.htm#fromView=search&page=3&position=8&uuid=7eed1900-db19-4bac-9443-f8513d4ef3a0&query=zodiac+signs

13 Designed by Macrovector on Freepik. https://www.freepik.com/free-vector/solar-system-astronomy-banner_4005076.htm#fromView=search&page=1&position=3&uuid=65c0ca4d-0ab7-4f6b-a8ff-bb64919372b5&query=solar+system

14 Designed by Macrovector on Freepik. https://www.freepik.com/free-vector/horoscope-infographic-set-with-zodiac-planet-symbols-flat-vector-illustration_58574559.htm#fromView=search&page=1&position=12&uuid=3ba50d9f-7538-48e3-8794-3f9b60e5fa05&query=12+houses+astrology

15 Designed by Nikitabuida on Freepik. https://www.freepik.com/free-photo/old-russian-book_1156398.htm#fromView=search&page=1&position=24&uuid=34a97cb4-928b-4b08-bf03-f4e10cce18d0&query=magical+library

16 Photo by Pixabay: https://www.pexels.com/photo/hanging-gold-colored-pendant-with-necklace-39239/

17 Photo by Pixabay: https://www.pexels.com/photo/close-up-of-hands-257037/

18 Photo by Marcus Aurelius: https://www.pexels.com/photo/woman-practicing-yoga-6787218/

19 Photo by Pixabay: https://www.pexels.com/photo/blue-water-68474/

20 https://www.pexels.com/photo/colored-light-waves-forming-a-pattern-3121766/

www.ingramcontent.com/pod-product-compliance
Lightning Source LLC
Chambersburg PA
CBHW072154200426
43209CB00052B/1195